HOMER LANE

AND THE LITTLE COMMONWEALTH

HOMER LANE
AND THE LITTLE COMMONWEALTH

E. T. BAZELEY

With an Introduction by
The Right Hon. The EARL OF LYTTON

SCHOCKEN BOOKS • NEW YORK

First published 1928

First SCHOCKEN PAPERBACK edition 1969

Published by arrangement with George Allen & Unwin Ltd.

Library of Congress Catalog Card No. 69–19624

Manufactured in the United States of America

INTRODUCTION

Miss Bazeley has said truly enough that knowledge of the existence of the Little Commonwealth caused the hearts of many to dance. There is, perhaps, no experience in life more stirring than the discovery for the first time that something hitherto believed to be an unattainable ideal has been proved to be a practical reality. This was the experience of those who visited the little colony which lived so short a life, yet revealed so great a truth, among the hills of Dorsetshire. Here was a prison without bolts or bars, a prison to which one condemned offender at least had been known to travel unaccompanied, of his own free will; a reformatory in which the inmates remained for the period of their sentence without compulsion or restraint, in which some even remained after their sentences had expired and to which others returned when they could, as to the home in which they found most happiness; a penal institution which left no stigma on those who passed through it, and whose occupants were returned to society not merely better than when they arrived, but actually better than many who spend their lives without ever breaking a law or coming into conflict with established authority. Miss Bazeley has drawn a faithful picture of some

of the features of this remarkable experiment from
the point of view of one who was a member of
the staff for a large part of its existence and who,
as such, shared in its daily activities and is entitled
to claim a measure of credit for its success.   Many
other accounts might be written, all differing
widely from each other in the point of view presented or in the incidents described, and yet each
might be an equally truthful account of the life
which was lived in those three or four cottages,
and of the reshaping of the young minds and
characters which went on there.   The essential
thing about the Little Commonwealth was that it
was a living community, the members of which
were changing, growing, developing from day to
day, and not an institution in which the same
routine, discipline and regulations were imposed
without variation upon all alike.   Different visitors,
therefore, on different days would find in the
community the most varying experiences.   It is
fortunate that the only account which has yet
been given to the world of this unique community
should come from one who knew it in all its
phases, in its constructive and destructive moods,
in its moments of crisis and in its uneventful
routine ; who knew most of the citizens from the
day of their arrival till the day of their departure
and personally witnessed the wonderful transforma-
tions through which they passed.   In addition to
her own personal narrative, Miss Bazeley has

placed in the Appendix a paper which deals with the emotional crisis which led to the closing of the school in 1918. All those, therefore, who have heard of the Little Commonwealth or visited it during its short existence, and many, perhaps, who have never heard of it before, will find in these pages a story of absorbing human interest. They will find also material for the study of a wholly unconventional method of dealing with those who, for various reasons, have declared war upon society and to whom society, without further discrimination, has given the comprehensive and erroneous title of "criminal."

The questions which will naturally occur to most readers of this book are : Why, if the Little Commonwealth was so successful, did it come to an end so prematurely ? Why, if its methods were so triumphantly vindicated, do we still rely upon punishment for the restraint of crime ? Why do we still send children to prison ? Why do we still attempt to reform the characters of the morally delinquent in institutions where they are subjected to the discipline of an established authority ? There can only be one answer to these questions. In one sense the Little Commonwealth failed, and it is worth while for those who hoped so much from its success, who had implicit faith in its methods, who knew the admirable quality of the human material which it turned out, to try to discover the reasons for its failure. It is to this problem that I shall devote the few comments that I desire to make by way of an introduction to Miss Bazeley's story.

The admission that the Little Commonwealth was a failure is not, of course, an admission that it failed as a reformatory, that it did not do for the boys and girls who were sent to it all that its friends hoped or expected of it. In this respect it succeeded more completely than its founders even believed possible. It failed only in establishing the general applicability of the principles on which it was conducted. It was, throughout its existence, and it still remains in the minds of many who knew of it, a freak institution associated with the influence of a unique personality. If one were to ask any of the children who passed through the Little Commonwealth and who are to-day upright and law-abiding citizens to what they attribute the change in their attitude towards society, I believe that most of them would reply: "It was Daddy that made me see things differently." If one had asked the teachers or reformatory superintendents who visited the Little Commonwealth whether they left it with a certainty that their own methods were wrong and that those of the Little Commonwealth were right, whether, in fact, their first act on returning to their own institutions had been to substitute the Commonwealth methods for their own, they would have replied, perhaps a little sadly: "No, we have seen a most wonderful and inspiring place, we are filled with admiration for the work of a most wonderful man, but we could not ourselves do what he is doing." Even Miss Bazeley, a member of the staff and a resident citizen of the Commonwealth, has given as the reason why visitors left with dancing hearts that they had discovered "a man"—more inspired and more sincere than any other man they had ever known. Here is the explanation of the failure. If the known success of the Little Commonwealth was due, as so many believed, to the personality of Homer Lane, then obviously it could not serve as a model reformatory, it was not worth keeping alive. If anything could make Mr. Lane angry, it was the assertion that he was "a wonderful man," or that the success of the Little Commonwealth was due to his personality. He felt such a statement to be the condemnation of the principles in which he believed, the stamp of failure on the work of his life, and it was his hard fate to hear such condemnation almost daily upon the lips of those who were his greatest admirers and the most enthusiastic upholders of his principles. It was because the members of the Managing Committee could not think of carrying on the Commonwealth without him, and because they had not sufficient courage to take the public into their confidence and tell the whole story of the circumstances leading up to and including the Home

Office inquiry, which was the only condition on which they could retain him, that they decided, in 1918, to close the Commonwealth. It was because Mr. Lane knew that all those from whom he might have expected support for his principles could not get away from his personality that he himself accepted the failure of the Little Commonwealth experiment and turned to other work. Yet Mr. George Montagu (now Lord Sandwich), the original founder of the Commonwealth, had conceived the idea and chosen the site for its establishment before he had heard of the existence of Mr. Lane. Mr. Lane's association with it was quite fortuitous, it could have been established without him, it could have been carried on without him, its principles could be applied to-day with equal success to every reformatory in the world. The only fact which differentiated Lane from all other men was not that he had better ideas than they, that he thought of things which other men did not think of, but that he really believed everything which he professed, and that, as Miss Bazeley has pointed out, he had the courage to put into practice every article of his faith among people to whom such faith was but a mischievous superstition. The results which excited the wonder of puzzled admirers were to Lane but the natural and inevitable consequence of the application of sound principles. He never had the slightest doubt what the consequences would be, provided that he had acted according to those principles which the experience of his life had taught him to be infallible, and it was the tragedy of his life that to the end men never said of him, " What admirable principles, let us adopt them," but always, " What a marvellous man, he is inimitable."

Of course, there are those who believe that the success of the Little Commonwealth was due to the genius of Homer Lane, and they will find ample confirmation of their belief in Miss Bazeley's story. For them the study of this experiment may be entertaining, but those alone can derive profit from such a study who are willing to believe that the principles which Lane applied so successfully in the Commonwealth are of universal application and would be equally successful wherever and whenever applied.

What, then, were those principles ?

First and foremost was the law of love. Lane genuinely believed that you can cure whatever you can love, and he consistently acted upon this principle. In holding this belief he showed no originality ; in the practice of it he was almost unique. Every Christian professes such a belief ; it is taught to almost every child in stories like " Beauty and the Beast " or " The Frog Prince," but Lane was alone both in his interpretation and his practice of the law of love. In his life the word "love " had a wholly different meaning from that which it has for most of us. It had for him no association with either sentiment or emotion. With most men, love means being fond of— affection; with Lane it meant being on the side of—approval, championship. Love in this sense, he always maintained, had been destroyed by the moralists, and man's best hope of salvation lay in its recovery. Many people might have been fond of the children who came to the Little Common- wealth, although they disapproved of their conduct; might, in fact, have claimed to love them, in spite of such disapproval. These people could never have effected the kind of cure which Lane produced in every case. Lane alone loved the children, not in spite of their crimes, but because of their crimes; nay, could even love, in his sense, the very crimes themselves, and thus he had no diffi- culty in curing them. What he did others could do equally, but always and only on condition that their love contained no element of pity, was genuinely synonymous with admiration, and took the form of sympathy with and championship of the very qualities of which society most strongly disapproved. It was this quality in Lane which most puzzled even those who knew him inti- mately, and probably my attempt to interpret it will be found equally puzzling. The idea of loving evil qualities, of championing evil-doers, of being on the side of law-breakers, is so funda- mentally at variance with the morality in which we are all brought up, that it seems at first to be incomprehensible. No one, I hope, will so mis-understand what I have written as to think I have attributed to Mr. Lane approval of the crimes which the young hooligans who were sent to the Little Commonwealth had committed, or a desire to see the latter continue in the career of crime on which they had started. What I have tried to explain is that he was able to see in those crimes evidence of qualities admirable in themselves and when differently expressed recognizable as the highest virtues; that when he heard the record of the evil the children had committed, instead of pitying them as poor little sinners, he could admire them as stout-hearted little ruffians. It was because of his genuine admiration for their high spirit, and his knowledge of the causes which had directed them into anti-social rather than social activities, that he was able to secure their complete con-fidence and substitute in their hearts a different set of ideals. This was the secret of his success, but the law on which he acted would lead anyone to similar results.

The second great principle—that of freedom—on which the work at the Little Commonwealth was based, was as much misunderstood as the first. Here again the originality lay not in the conception but in the application of the prin-ciple. Since the dawn of creation man has valued freedom, has sought after it, struggled for it, professed faith in it and denied it to his fellow-men. When Rousseau roused his generation with the words, " Man is born free," he was expressing what everyone wished to be true but knew to be false. When visitors turned their backs on the Little Commonwealth and went home with dancing hearts, they perhaps said to themselves : " Here at last we have found a community in which everyone is free to do as he pleases." If so, they had failed to appreciate the most important lesson which the Commonwealth had to teach. The conception of the Little Commonwealth as a reformatory in which there was no compulsion is completely erroneous. That the compulsion was of a different kind from that which is to be found in other reformatory or penal institutions is true enough, but compulsion was there all the same. Indeed, the chief function of the Commonwealth was to teach its citizens that there is no such thing in human affairs as absolute freedom and that no man in life can escape responsibility for the consequences of his own actions. The great merit of the institution, and the fact which differentiated it from all other institutions of the kind, was that the compulsion experienced by its inmates was only of the rational and inevitable type which would be met with in the world outside, namely, an economic compulsion. It was not the arbitrary compulsion of an individual authority. One of the wisest provisions of the Little Commonwealth was that which required the citizens to do the work which the needs of their community demanded, and which paid them wages for the work so done. Every citizen started in debt for the clothes supplied to him and for the food he consumed. Until he acquired sufficient skill to earn his own keep he was a charge on the household in which he lived, and his initial debt to the community was deducted from his earnings before his own account could stand in credit. This genuine economic foundation for the life of the community was of supreme importance and, more than anything else, perhaps, taught the children to form sound ideas regarding the value of labour, of money and of property. The freedom which existed in the Commonwealth was not the absolute freedom which is found only in the minds of poets and anarchists, but the limited freedom both of the individual and of the community to make mistakes, to test for themselves the value of every law and the necessity for every restraint imposed upon them.

The third important principle which characterized the Little Commonwealth was the principle of self-government—the right of the inmates to make their own laws and themselves to elect the authority they agreed to obey. Yet again the originality lay less in the principle itself than in its application, and the only remarkable feature in this connection was the thoroughness with which it was applied. Lane did not believe in a restricted application of a principle if the principle itself was sound, and he knew the danger of showing freedom to a community and then withholding it.   The inmates of each cottage made the rules which governed the life within the cottage, fixed their own time-table and enforced their own discipline.   Similarly, the whole community made and enforced the laws which governed the community life.   The effect of this principle was to break down the anti-social attitude of the delinquent child, to eliminate the possibility of securing the approval of the group by a courageous defiance of authority.   At the Little Commonwealth there was no authority to defy except the authority of the whole community, and no group to appeal to in defying that authority.   In this school the law-breakers not only learnt to become law-makers, they learnt also to become law-enforcers, and the whole of their activities were turned into social channels.

These were the main principles which distinguished the Little Commonwealth from other reformatories, though, as Miss Bazeley's story will show, there were many subtle features in the technique employed by Lane in his relationship with individual citizens which may be said to have contributed to the success of his work. Whether or not co-education should be included among the essential principles of the Commonwealth is a debatable point.   The inclusion of both boys and girls in the scheme was considered by its original authors to be essential—Lane himself would certainly have maintained that the presence of each sex was necessary to the re-education or normal development of the other—and the experience of five years proved that they were right. But this feature was rather an educational panacea than a fundamental principle of a reformatory institution, and I cannot place it in quite the same category as the other three principles.

I have said enough, I hope, to show that the Little Commonwealth was not an inimitable institution, the product of a single genius, but a model reformatory the principles of which could be applied with equal success to other institutions for the reformation of adult criminals as well as in the treatment of delinquent children. The only requisites are a correct appreciation of the conditions of its success and an application of them with a sincerity equal to that with which they were applied at Batcombe. So long, however, as public opinion maintains a belief in the efficacy of punishment and the discipline of personal authority, so long must the teaching of Homer Lane, as illustrated in the Little Commonwealth, be described as a failure.

In her description of the central and all-pervading personality at the Commonwealth, Miss Bazeley has said one thing which all who knew Mr. Lane will recognize as both true and puzzling : he could never explain or defend himself. His sympathy and capacity for understanding others amounted to genius. No erring mortal or social misfit could wish for a better advocate, but whenever his own conduct or opinions were in question, he seemed to take an almost fiendish pleasure in misrepresenting himself and encouraging the mistaken opinion which others had formed of him. If any of his friends ventured to intervene and attempt a justification of him, he would be sure to resent the action and disown the proffered explanation. In reality one of the simplest and most obvious of men, so that those who really knew him could always foretell what he would say or do in any circumstances, he remained to the end, to all but a few intimates, an *homme incompris*, an enigma, a mystery. It was not surprising, therefore, that to the official world he appeared more Devil than God, that they misunderstood both his actions and his motives, that they pursued him for years and eventually banished him from the country as an " undesirable alien." Can the Home Office be blamed for not understanding a man who puzzled even his friends ?

When the crisis occurred in the Commonwealth in 1918 and the Home Office proposed to hold an inquiry into the circumstances, the Managing Committee welcomed the proposal and stipulated only that the person or persons deputed to hold the inquiry should be of a mentality capable of understanding so unconventional a place as the

Little Commonwealth, and so unconventional a
man as Homer Lane. It would have been impossible to discover any man less qualified for the
purpose than the one actually selected by the
Home Secretary. Mr. Rawlinson, on the first day
of the inquiry, announced with obvious relish that,
as Recorder of Cambridge, he had had twenty
years' experience of the sordid side of human
life, that there was no vice or crime with which
he was not intimately familiar, and that he was
not a man, therefore, whom it was worth while
to try and bamboozle! It was a fatal opening.
At the sound of those words the devil of contra-
diction seemed to enter into Homer Lane, and
for the next few weeks he set himself to bamboozle
Mr. Rawlinson. In this task he was only too
successful. He completely satisfied this unfortunate
man that the Little Commonwealth was a sink of
iniquity, that the love which the Superintendent
bore to the children confided to his care was
purely sexual, and that the story of an assault told
by the runaway girls was simply true! Rawlinson
believed in evil with as much sincerity as Lane
believed in good. Each spent many years of his
life in listening to the defence of others and
judging their actions. It would have been equally
hard for a bad man to convince Lane that he was
not really good or for a good man to convince
Rawlinson that he was not really bad. Both
have now passed beyond the veil, and it is good

to think of their meeting again before another tribunal, where the secrets of all hearts are revealed, where neither sarcasm, suspicion, insinuation nor paradox can obscure the truth. Will their rôles be reversed and each find in the other the best advocate of himself? One can almost hear their simultaneous exclamation, "How right you were!" One thing, at least, is certain, that in that meeting there will be no reproaches, not even probably any prolonged explanation, for the conditions of the meeting will be such as never existed and never could exist on earth. If, as Thoreau said, "it takes two to speak the truth, one to speak and the other to hear," then to speak truth to one who will only hear falsehood is no better than to tell a lie. This, perhaps, was what prevented the Managing Committee in 1918 from taking the only course which would have been just to Mr. Lane and saved the Little Commonwealth. They could have saved the Commonwealth and sacrificed Lane, but this would have been a manifest injustice to an innocent man of which they were incapable. To have kept Mr. Lane and carried on the Commonwealth without the Home Office certificate necessitated the publication of the whole truth. The statement which now appears in the Appendix to this book was prepared with this object. At the last moment, however, other counsels prevailed and the majority of the Committee, in the mistaken belief that this sacrifice was necessary in justice to Mr. Lane, chose the alternative of closing the Commonwealth. The great work was suspended, to the despair of all who had grounded their hopes of penal reform on the rock of its foundation ; and the truth which, if given full publicity in 1918, would soon have lost all interest or mystery, acquired, as a skeleton in the cupboard, all the secrecy and zest of a scandal. Friends were mystified, critics were shocked, and a damaging weapon was placed in the hands of the police when, in 1925, they made his technical offence under the Aliens Act of failure to notify them of a change of address the excuse to blacken Lane's character and secure his removal from the country. It was a tragic mistake, only to be explained, I suggest, by the fear that the public would not at that time hear truth when it was told. Whether in this respect the Committee judged rightly or wrongly, the consequences of their action have been different from what they hoped. An injustice was all unwittingly done, not only to Mr. Lane, but also to that large section of the public which was capable of hearing the truth, which believed fervently in the principles of the Little Commonwealth and which has never been able to understand why it was closed. This injustice Miss Bazeley has helped to remove. Her book, with another which is being published under the title of *Talks to Parents and Teachers*, by Homer

Lane, should give to those who may care to study them not only help in the difficulties of their own lives, but a clearer conception of a man who was so simple that only children could understand him, so good that his worth was more apparent to the foolish than to the wise, so generous that no one could injure him, so modest that no one could praise him, so trusting that no one could deceive him, so happy that nothing could depress him, so great that no one could for long feel small in his presence.

LYTTON.

GOVERNOR'S CAMP, BENGAL.
   October 1926.

CONTENTS

NOTE.—I have given fictitious names to all the citizens and to some of the other people in this book.

E. T. B.

HOMER LANE
AND THE LITTLE COMMONWEALTH

CHAPTER I

THE ORIGIN OF THE COMMONWEALTH AND THE HISTORY OF THE FIRST MONTHS

" Those who will dare all, give all, bear all, have the power to re-create the whole life and character of other men."

TWELVE years ago [1] the Little Commonwealth came as a great hope to many of us who were engaged upon educational work of all kinds with young people. It not only gave us hope, it gave us courage, the courage that comes from seeing our convictions realized. If with hopeful steps we climbed the Dorsetshire hills which led to the Commonwealth, most of us came away with dancing hearts, for we had discovered a man who not only had a greater and more scientific belief than is commonly to be met with, but one who carried out his belief more daringly and more sanely than we had thought possible.

We expected to find an original theory being practised by that awe-inspiring being, the educational expert; we found instead a way of life

[1] This book was begun in 1926.

which all might follow, inviting, challenging, elemental and inclusive. It dawned upon us, from Mr. Lane's conversations, that no expert knowledge or training, no superior powers were needed ; all that was required was to make a beginning and to step out upon the same adventurous path without too much anxious looking before or after.

A first visit to the Commonwealth was to some of us like our first glimpse of the Alps. We always knew that these would be beautiful, but we needed the direct sight of them to make us realize how beautiful and how real they actually were. Just, too, as one felt after seeing the mountains, that the return to them would be made again and again, so one knew that one would return again and again to the Commonwealth. The life of mountaineers is not, however, an easy one, nor is it without danger.

At the Commonwealth and in Mr. Lane's later work, great possibilities seemed to be expanding for all of us. Then came the newspaper reports of his trial in 1925, bringing doubt and disappointment to some who were ignorant of what had been really happening. Could it be that those bright possibilities which had been shaping themselves into realities were nothing, after all, but a false and passing mirage ?

To all those who have thus felt themselves in doubt I would answer that the work of the Little

Commonwealth was solid, it was sound all through, there was nothing flimsy or shoddy in it. It was an inspired and inspiring bit of work. It was equally great and equally illuminating both in what it achieved and in what it stopped short of achieving. There was so much of vitality and of sensitiveness in the life there that the experience of it was like a thought flashing out of the common things of life and giving one a new, a stark and a more significant set of values.

It is a picture of the daily life of this little community that I shall endeavour to paint and of the man who, by his daring, his endurance and his generosity of spirit set those who lived there on a new way of life.

ORIGIN

The Little Commonwealth was a farm community of some fifty people; it consisted of eight or nine little ones, varying in age from nine months to nine years, four or five grown-ups, and thirty-eight or so boys and girls of ages between fourteen and eighteen. The latter had been sent to us either by magistrates or by parents who found them unmanageable at home. The red roofs of our houses are still to be seen on the green slope of the Dorsetshire Downs between Evershot and Sherborne.

The story of our origin is, I believe, briefly as

follows. Early in this century there was a movement in the United States among those interested in prison reform for the formation of new sorts of communities for delinquent young people. Instead of sending young hooligans to prison they were sent to a junior republic, where they were given responsibility to organize the affairs of themselves and their community as a miniature state. These miniature republics were so successful and seemed to offer so many possibilities for the making of good citizens that Mr. George Montagu[1] in this country was asked to visit America and report on the possibility of the same kind of community being started for English youngsters. Mr. Montagu came back so much impressed by what he had seen that his uncle, the Earl of Sandwich, offered an unoccupied farm in Dorsetshire, Flowers Farm, as a ground for experimenting with an English Little Commonwealth. A Committee was formed of people interested in penal reform and in modern ideals of education. Hearing, at a later date, of Mr. Lane's work in the Ford Republic in America, some members of this Committee asked him to come across to England and advise them on certain points in connection with the little community they desired to found. Mr. Lane came in 1913, and in the sequel he stayed to carry out the work and did not return to America.

[1] In 1916, on the death of his uncle, Mr. Montagu became the Earl of Sandwich.

Mrs. Lane and his family followed before the end of 1913.

The Ford Republic had been a community for boys only. As a result of his observations while working there, Mr. Lane had decided that there must be girls in the next community as well as boys. It was inadvisable to make a beginning with boys and girls, raw from the streets, simultaneously, but should the new community be started by boys or by girls? Mr. Lane knew that if boys of fourteen or fifteen started the new community they would resent the addition later on of girls to their gang, whereas if girls started the community they would be perfectly ready when the moment came to admit boys to the circle. Consequently he asked one of the interested magistrates to send him three or four girls. The first candidates were described as being not at all bad girls; they had been led astray by others stronger than themselves. This, however, was not the type of girl needed for building a new community. Mr. Lane needed, not those who followed a lead, but those who took the lead, positive people of strong character, contra-suggestible rather than suggestible.

I give below the story of the first months of the Commonwealth in Mr. Lane's words. The account is taken from one of his lectures given at South Kensington in March 1916.[1]

---

[1] The lecture will be found in full in *Four Lectures on Childhood: The Age of Loyalty*, edited by Rev. H. H. Symonds (Pub.).

EARLY HISTORY

Mr. Cecil Chapman, Magistrate of the Tower Bridge Police Court, had invited me to attend his court for the purpose of securing the nucleus of the population of the Commonwealth. Passing the door of an anteroom on my way to the court room, I heard angry voices, and through the door saw a policeman struggling with three girls. One of them struck the officer a vicious blow with her fist, and the language was anything but appropriate to the precincts of a court. After several cases had been heard, these three girls, thirteen, fourteen and fifteen years of age, were ushered into the court room, and by dint of considerable pushing by the officers, punctuated by smothered protests in their native language, the girls were placed in the prisoners' box. Then was related a story of misbehaviour and wrong-doing that was thrilling. The three girls had for months been under the surveillance of the police. They were systematic shoplifters, so clever in their operations that evidence sufficient to secure conviction was difficult to obtain. They were well known to the police and had conducted their operations over a wide area.

A representative of the school authorities, speaking from notes, gave a detailed story of their disturbing influences in the school, and enumerated the number of times and occasions for corporal punishment. There was no reason to think the

parents were in any way to blame for the girls'
wrong-doing, for they seemed very much disturbed as the story of the girls' misdemeanours
was unfolded.

The girls themselves stood sullenly listening to
the proceedings. Once the smallest, turning and
seeing her mother weeping behind her, began to
cry, when her companion nudged her and whispered
audibly, " Don't be a fool. Stare 'em out."

They were certainly not very promising material.
In the course of the testimony the officer related
the following incident. When the girls were
arrested in the act of secreting some stolen articles,
one of them had said : " I'll come along and own
up if you'll let that girl go," indicating a fourth
and younger member of the group. At this point
I determined to try to get these girls for the
Commonwealth. Sitting beside the magistrate, I
whispered my request. " Oh no. They are much
too bad for the Commonwealth. They must be
rigidly restrained," he replied.

I could only repeat my request and urge that
these were just the sort of children that would
ensure the successful organization of the Commonwealth.

Finally the prisoners were remanded for a week
for further discussion as to their future.

At this point I wish to testify my great admiration
for the magistrate. In finally consenting that the
girls might become members of the new and untried

community, he ignored the insistent advice and gloomy, fearful predictions of each and every one of his assistants.

Nor was he helped to this decision by the girls themselves, who repelled, sullenly and insolently, any friendly advances on his part. I have always suspected that in finally agreeing to place the girls in my care he was influenced by a desire to rid the court of four undesirables. I fear that my insistence was unreasonable. I am sure he had no great confidence in the likelihood of a sudden change of heart on the part of the girls, for in committing them to my care he also placed at my disposal two constables and a police matron to help get them safely to the Commonwealth. I did not, however, avail myself of the assistance of the officers, for I dared not risk losing the girls. I preferred to depend on their own good sportsmanship.

On the appointed day I went to the place where they were detained, and in spite of the amazed protest of the matron, set off single-handed with my three desperate criminals for the Little Commonwealth.

Needless to say, when our train drew out from Paddington an hour later, the girls were safely aboard, in spite of the fact that they had had abundant opportunity to escape. In fact, they could not have escaped, because there was no one to escape from. I did not even stay with them to watch them. Thus their first contact with the Commonwealth was that of responsibility and confidence.

I would like to describe minutely the lives of these children during the next few days, if our time would allow of it. How, one by one, their virtues budded and blossomed out in their new environment. But when, after a fortnight, Mr. Cecil Chapman came to visit us, these children, who had insolently repulsed his friendly advances in the court, now captured him as he was descending from his carriage, and bore him off to see their garden, their house, their home, and, arm-in-arm, brought him back again, with wild flowers protruding from every buttonhole of his coat.

His first question was : " What have you done that has made these dreadful, hardened criminals into such delightful, free, natural children ? " And then we quarrelled !

I insisted that it was none of me, nor of my assistants, and not even of the place itself, but the nature of all children that he saw.

We still sometimes disagree on this point. I have described these girls in such detail for the purpose of showing you the sort of children that have become citizens of the Little Commonwealth. As interesting a story could be told of nearly every one of the fifty citizens that have contributed to the growth of our community, whether boys or girls.

For two weeks or thereabouts the girls were in sole possession of the Commonwealth. There was no government, no authority, and none needed. After the first day or two the girls naturally assumed a share in the work of the house. The matron, a motherly woman, with no experience of institutional work, accepted their help gratefully, but did not demand it. Then, as the girls began to make inquiries as to when others were coming, it was decided that we were ready to take in boys. I must admit that I shared to some extent the matron's fears that with the coming of the boys the peace of our little family would be shattered, but for a different reason. She was a firm disbeliever in co-education and could not see how we were to prevent adolescent human nature from its traditional tendencies. I knew that our peace was the peace of stagnation and that boys were less apt than girls to be influenced by the beauties of nature, the lovely hills and flowers and spaces of the country, and there would probably be the necessity for the introduction of some form of authority to limit the scope of their experiments.

On the day of the boys' arrival the girls had enthusiastically prepared for their coming. They provided a nice tea, decorated the dining-room and set two tables, one for the boys and one for the girls, of course. The flowers and the nicest cakes were on the boys' table, also of course. When starting for the station to meet the boys, a three-mile walk, the girls timidly asked if they might go too. I cordially consented. We stood on the platform as the train drew up, in a group. Five boys, swaggering and laughing boisterously, smoking cigarettes, dirty and unkempt, alighted (noisily). The girls at once retreated. When we started for the Commonwealth the girls were a long way in advance of the boys and myself, walking quickly, as though anxious to avoid being overtaken. When about half-way home the girls were lingering slightly, and as we neared the Commonwealth, I saw one of the girls turn and wave her hand, which signal was answered by several boys. That broke the ice. As we approached the house one of the girls and her boy companion had lingered in the rear, engaged in conversation. The matron called my attention to this at once as a confirmation of her predictions, but I persuaded her to ignore this dreadful breach of conventionality for the moment. A little later she came again for advice. One of the girls had asked her if she might sit next one of the boys at tea (so far as I know this was the first time that an authority had been consulted since the girls came). The matron seemed annoyed at my care-lessness in recommending that the request be granted. The meal was not exactly a success from the hostess's point of view, but was gone through without incident. Then the girls cleared away and the boys went out to look over their new surroundings. They returned quite late, with the stain of ripe strawberries on their faces, and surreptitiously offered the girls some of the fruit from their pockets. The girls came to me and complained that these horrid boys had been stealing the strawberries. I sympathized with their views but, much to their disgust, declined to take action. That night there was a good deal of noise in the boys' wing of the house, which lasted until late. Both the matron and the girls appealed to me to stop it, but without result. Then things began to go badly. We were no longer a peaceful, orderly family. The boys were cheeky, noisy and destructive. They did no work, but swaggered about defiantly. The girls had now become sufficiently acquainted with them to remonstrate vigorously for their hooliganism. They criticized the boys' table manners, their behaviour at night and their laziness and lack of interest. The girl who had requested the privilege of sitting beside a boy, now changed her seat and returned to the girls' table, explaining that the way James ate his soup spoiled her appetite. The romance was shattered. The relationship between the boys and the girls became more strained each day, the boys purposely annoying the girls and the girls becoming more resentful and disapproving. I was asked repeatedly to take the boys in hand and stop their undesirable activities; but I refused, insisting that it was not my function to act as policeman. I explained my position in the presence of the boys as follows : " We came here to do as we liked, and so long as we liked to break windows, yell, take fruit and live at the expense of others, we would do so. If at any time we felt like doing something else that was more fun, we would do that."

The girls and my adult assistants made their disapproval of me and my attitude quite evident.

Finally, however, the noise at night became intolerable. My male assistant, no longer in sympathy with my views of freedom, finally, at the request of the feminine portion of the family, decided to put a stop to this disgraceful row. He secured a stout stick from the hedge and with this in hand begged the boys to be more considerate of the others in the house and to retire quietly. He did not unduly draw attention to the stick in his hand, but implied that he had resources at his disposal that would be called into play if the noise continued. That night the noise was as bad as ever and the resources were called into play. Each night it seemed to get worse, in spite of vigorous measures to prevent it.

I wish to say here that the noise could have been stopped by a very simple and proven method. Had my assistant joined in the noise-making, he would have extracted all the fun from it, and it would have ceased. But I did not enlighten him, for I wanted the noise to continue until it got so bad that the whole community would be up in arms. I wanted the entire group to assume responsibility. As the efforts of my assistant became more vigorous, so did those of the boys. One night, after a particularly trying din had been going on, and the man with the stick had failed to find anyone awake when he went to stop it, I went to the boys' landing to see if it were possible to create such an uproar without serious damage to the furniture and the house.

As my footsteps were heard on the stairs, the noise ceased instantly. I went from room to room to see if the furniture was being mistreated, and in each room the occupant was soundly and sweetly sleeping. But in one of the rooms my identity was discovered by its occupant, who at once jumped from his bed and shouted, "It's all right, boys, it's only Mr. Lane." I was greatly pleased, for I now knew that I had been admitted to the inner circle, and was in a position to begin my part of the work.

May I again repeat that I am describing my part in the organization of the Commonwealth, because in the previous papers I have made many critical comments about parental relationship. The prominence I am giving myself in this story is that you may see how small is the part I have taken in regulation of the affairs of the community.

My function has been to encourage all activity, bad as well as good.

About this time we were planning new cottages for the accommodation of more citizens. In the cottage in which we lived at the time of my story, each boy was provided with a separate bedroom, while in the girls' wing two or more beds were placed in larger rooms. I may add that this was accidental, not by design. I had noticed that certain boys, being unused to the quietness of a Dorset night, had, for companionship's sake, moved their beds into another's room and were sleeping double, as they called it. This gave me the opportunity I had been watching for to give the whole group some responsibility for a community decision.

I asked the boys and girls if they would help me decide an important matter. We met after tea.

I produced the plans of the new cottage and showed them that separate rooms had been provided for each person, both boys and girls. I stated that, as the cost of building was much greater if constructed with separate rooms than if dormitories were installed, I presumed that, since the boys preferred to sleep together in the same room, we might now alter the plans and not provide the separate rooms.

I proposed doing this and asked if they approved. After a momentary pause, surprised that they should be consulted on a matter of such importance, they began to venture their opinions, modestly and timidly at first, but as differences of opinion were expressed, the timidity disappeared. Having successfully started the quarrel, I withdrew to a safe and remote corner. The hubbub was great. All were talking at the same time, the one with the largest lung capacity being the object of the combined attacks of the others. Soon they appealed to me to put the loudest-voiced boy out because he was a disturber. I refused. Then gradually individual opinions were heard. They had already begun to discuss matters other than separate rooms. True to my conviction that discovery is an essential element in the assumption of responsibility, I waited patiently until they should realize the futility of discussion without organization, and was rewarded when the biggest boy stood in the middle of the room and, with clenched fist, threatened anyone who interrupted him. His parliamentary triumph was but momentary, however. He was soon deprived of the privilege of the floor. Finally, one of the girls suggested that someone should be chosen to run the meeting. This was done. A policeman was appointed. I want to call your attention to the fact that this group of children, when given responsibility for their own affairs, chose a policeman with preventive powers rather than a chairman to give privileges. It was the business of the chosen leader to keep eleven people quiet while one talked. The meeting, however, having solved the preliminary problems of organization, soon resolved itself into an orderly, deliberative body.

It was finally decided that separate rooms were to be retained in the future cottages. One of the girls summed up the whole matter in a decisive speech, short, terse, but quite as much to the point as it could have been expressed in a convention of doctors and psychologists in these words : " If you don't sleep good at night, the next day your face is all crinkled up and you get into rows all day." This view, which was accepted and applauded, finally impressed one of the group as being contrary to the habit of the boys in indulging in their nightly noise-making enterprise. The matter was discussed. Having already decided that no boys should double up in bed, it was but a step further to vote to decide that making a noise after ten o'clock was detrimental to the public good.

The question of bathing was taken up and other matters pertaining to personal comfort and welfare.

Now at this, the first meeting of the Little Commonwealth, the decisions of the majority were accepted and adopted by all, even the minority. For the child is loyal to *his* public opinion spontaneously.

These decisions were not called laws. In fact, they were not called at all. They were accepted without a label. Nor was there even a suggestion that the girls should not have the privilege of voicing their opinions and voting. That came later, after labels were affixed to the meetings. These meetings became frequent, one being called nearly every evening to discuss some matter pertaining to the intimate affairs of the little community. Soon it became apparent that some system of recording decisions was necessary, for at each meeting there was some violation of decisions previously made, under discussion, and the excuse usually given was that the matter had been forgotten. Also frequent dispute arose as to the exact meaning of decisions.

Then another difficulty arose and was solved by discussion. The business regulating the affairs of the group was always delayed by discussions of violations of previous decisions, so that it became increasingly difficult to get through the business. It was decided to divide the business of the community into two different kinds and to hold meetings on alternate evenings for each. Thus the judicial was created as distinct from the legislative. One of the girls was chosen to preside over the judicial meetings, but as yet these had not been called " courts." In the midst of one of them, however, someone used the word " court " and referred to the chairman as a magistrate. Almost instantly the character of the meeting changed. The boy whose evasions were under discussion, and who had up to that moment been on the defensive, changed places with the girl judge. Public opinion was with the boy and against the judge and the law.

The witnesses lied valiantly in the interests of the boy defendant and disorder and horseplay broke up the meeting. Afterwards the boys said that no girl had a right to sit in judgment upon a boy, and the girls agreed. The girl judge resigned. What a comment upon the child's attitude towards our adult courts this is !

For several days there was no court held, but when things began to go badly again it was seen that the court must be reorganized in the interests of peace and the welfare of the community. Then a boy was chosen as judge, but in recognition of certain qualities that would remove the taint of association with our adult courts. The very boy who had the least regard for law and order and the conventions of society was elected to fill the judicial chair. I was amazed and disappointed, for I did not yet see all that was involved in these events. However, I preserved outward calm and watched. The court again took up its work, and I was amazed at the ability of the judge and his loyalty to the laws. Within a few weeks, however, this boy was impeached in his office and deposed because he himself furnished the greater number of cases for his own court and obviously could not judge himself. The original girl judge was then re-elected and presided with remarkable ability over the court for three terms.

It is obviously quite impossible for me to complete the story of the Little Commonwealth in such detail as I have described the events of the first few weeks, much as I should like to do so and helpful as such a description would be to our understanding of the age of loyalty. But our time forbids. You will be able to see what progress has been made in the two and a half years since the work was organized, by reading the report of the Little Commonwealth for the last year. But with these incidents as the starting-point, the citizens had assumed entire responsibility for the organization of their government. The standards which they have set for themselves and which they have enforced so cleverly through the machinery of their government are of such a character that many visitors to the Commonwealth express their conviction that there is some influence at work in the community quite external to the untutored impulses of the children and that this influence is really responsible for these standards. Now I will readily admit that this is true, but I insist that the influence is of a sort that the schoolmaster would characterize as demoralizing. I maintain that if the group of children in the Commonwealth had arrived at the age of loyalty without undue interference with their freedom, their standards would have been even higher than those that now prevail. The influence under which they come in the Commonwealth is one of encouragement, not of their good activities alone, but also of their bad ones. The foundations of society as represented by a public sentiment that is based upon economic law, as in the Commonwealth, being sound, it is perfectly safe to encourage all activity, both good and bad. If an effort does not realize its purpose and result in success, that effort will not be repeated.

Let me illustrate again the application of that influence. A boy of sixteen, loud-voiced, boastful, self-confident, joined the community. By virtue of a heavy and skilful fist he soon had a small group of admirers among the newer boys. His great boast was that he never took a dare. Public sentiment through the laws and courts failed to tone him down, noticeably because of his followers. He became the leader of the opposition to public sentiment. I had tried to divert his energy through the economic affairs of the community. He would work energetically at shovelling or any rough labour, but would not attempt any skilled work, such as bricklaying or carpentering. His ideals were based upon brute strength. Finally, the court applied extreme measures to regulate his activities, with the result that he grew worse and more defiant. At this point there was some discussion as to the desirability of establishing a prison for the confinement of such persons. I realized that here, obviously, was the place for some authority to step in and subdue the unruly spirit.

I was sitting next him at tea. "Why," I asked him, "do you make so much trouble here?" "I don't like the place," he replied. "Why not?" "Oh, it's too sissy and soft for me." "Why don't you run away then?" "It's no use, I'd only be caught and sent back." "Then why don't you change the place so you will like it?" "I would in a minute, if I could," he answered sullenly. "Where would you begin?" After a moment's thought he blurted out, "Right here. I'd smash up all these fussy tea-things, they're for women." "All right," I replied, handing him the poker from the fire-place, "go ahead and smash them." He hesitated, startled by the audacity of my proposal. We now had quite an audience of interested spectators. One of the boys said in a characteristic tone, "That's done it," meaning that at least one braggart had taken a dare. The boy was stung by the tone of this comment and, raising the poker, struck his tea-cup, smashing it to atoms. He then, somewhat awed by his own daring, assumed a somewhat defensive attitude towards me, but I smiled encouragingly upon him and placed another dish in readiness for destruction. "Go on," I encouraged cheerfully. Again the poker descended, amidst the applause of our audience. Again I pushed a plate towards him, and again and again, each one of which he smashed. But now one of the girls cried, "Shame, Mr. Lane,

you're making him do it." " Well, it's worth it," I
replied. " He's altering the Commonwealth so
that he will like it." " No," protested the boy,
" it isn't that, but you dared me to smash them."
" Yes, that's true," said the others.

" All right," said I, " we're both having our
fun. Let's finish the whole lot," and I placed
another plate in front of him. He hesitated, looked
helplessly round into the faces of the surrounding
group and finally struck it weakly. The others,
now utterly disgusted with the scene, pulled him
away and forcibly relieved him of the poker,
meantime voicing their entire disapproval of me.
This left him the victor in our contest of endurance.
He now assumed his original bravado, and from
the safety of the restraining arms of his friends,
with eyes blazing with excitement, declared, " No
one can dare me and get away with it." " But,"
I taunted, " you have stopped, here are more."
But at this the others protested. " No; let him
alone, he's had enough, and we'll have to pay for
the damage done." I could not answer this final
argument, for it was true. The dishes must be
replaced by the family. But I was determined to
see the thing through, especially as I now saw
that if the matter were left here the boy would
have won a triumph and been confirmed in his
bravado. So, having been convinced that I must
not further risk property at the expense of others,
I handed my gold watch to the boy. " Anyway,

I can dare you to smash my own watch," I said pleasantly, thrusting it into his reluctant hand. No one spoke, the others were speechless with astonishment. The boy looked frightened, hesitated, and held the watch to me, with frightened eyes. " I dare you to smash it," I said. Someone laughed and, his eyes blazing with fury, the boy raised the watch to send it crashing to the floor, but paused, hand in air, as he realized what he was about to do. " Go on," I encouraged smilingly. " I won't." " But you never take a dare." " I won't do it," doggedly. " All right, you know what you have called others who would not take a dare." " What ? " " A coward." " I'm not a coward," furiously. " There's the watch." " I won't smash it !" he cried, leaving the room. Then I heard again the very expressive remark, " That's done it ! "

The next day James applied for work as a bricklayer. In a half-bantering way I asked him why he now wanted to take up work he had refused before. He replied, with a whimsical smile : " I've got to earn more money to pay for those dishes you broke." When he left the Commonwealth to enlist in the Army he was judge of the citizens' court.

In the incident I have described he worked off his delayed self-assertive tendencies and caught up with himself and with his new social responsibilities. I am of the opinion that this incident was the critical turning-point in his life and that a future criminal was saved to society. May I quote a newspaper clipping that was sent to me from his home town :

TRIBUTE TO THE LITTLE COMMONWEALTH.

In a letter to Mr. B—— (a Probation Officer), Rifleman James H——, of the 2nd Battalion Rifle Brigade, now in France, states : "I am glad to say that the Little Commonwealth has made a man of me, and it is a debt that can never be repaid back. I am sure that if any of the other fellows were like me they would ask to be sent there. I had the best time of my life while I was at the Commonwealth." He adds that he has been in one charge that he would never forget. He was fortunate enough to come through without a scratch, while men were falling on his right and left. One of his best chums was shot right through the neck, and he bandaged his wound, which, however, proved fatal.[1]

I have related this incident to show you the nature of parental relationship in the Commonwealth and to indicate to you what, in my opinion, is the duty of the parent. It is this : To encourage all experiments of the child and assist him in reaching such conclusions as he will adopt as his own, so that he may, by the process of elimination, discard futile and false ideals.

Now one more incident to illustrate the remarkable understanding that is always in evidence among children. This incident will also show

[1] James was killed in France at a later date.—E. T. B.

why the citizens have not followed the precedent of the larger community and established a prison as an aid to civilization. It will show that children are much more scientific in their treatment of offenders than we adults are.

One of the boys was a great problem in the community : he was always before the court for some error of omission or commission. He could not keep out of trouble. All the penalties available to the judge had been imposed upon him, but without avail. He became sullen and defiant. He refused to work, and purposely committed acts in defiance of the laws. He became what in the greater world community would be called an habitual and confirmed criminal and would have been sent to prison. It was upon a girl judge that the responsibility for his future relationship with the community fell. Week after week Ted got deeper and deeper into trouble. During one of the court sessions, after complaint upon complaint had been brought against the unruly, defiant lad, the girl judge, realizing the futility of future penalties, arrived at this decision in the case. (Let me explain that Ted's mother had recently visited the Commonwealth and won the respect of every citizen by her gentle ways.) This was the judicial finding in the case :

" No boy would act as Ted does if he had not forgotten his mother. It is of no use punishing him, for it only makes him worse. He has lost his self-respect. What he needs is to get acquainted with his mother again and get his self-respect back. I shall send him home for a week's holiday at the expense of the taxpayers." Ted, who up to now had been a triumphant hero, hard and defiant, now burst into tears. He spent his week at home and returned a changed boy. The important part of this incident is that the judge ordered that the mother should not be informed that Ted was not enjoying a well-earned holiday, and that before his visit was over Ted had himself told his mother of the circumstances under which he was at home. This was a girl judge. We have had both boys and girls as judges and have had an opportunity to compare the relative qualities of each sex in a judicial capacity. Without any prejudice, I have arrived at the conclusion that in the Commonwealth the girl judge is the most skilful in treating offenders against the laws. The difference in method is that the girl, true to instinct, makes her decisions with reference to the effect upon the offender, often ignoring the law, to find exactly the right action to take, while the boy judge has the law and the letter of the law in his mind, to the exclusion of its effect opon the offender. Can anyone doubt the capacity of the citizens to govern themselves in view of the recent compulsory education law which they have enacted? The law requires: " That every citizen shall attend school two hours each day until he can satisfactorily pass an examination of a certain defined grade." This law imposes upon themselves two hours' school work, in addition to a full working day spent in their different manual occupations. I could wish for more of your time in order that I might try to convince you that we borrow much unnecessary trouble by not allowing greater scope for the activities of our children.

CHAPTER II

EDUCATIONAL FORCES IN THE LITTLE COMMONWEALTH

Relationship between Citizens and Grown-up Helpers. The Family

It will be observed, from the preceding chapter, that the chance collection of boys and girls at Flowers Farm developed into a community through the necessity for a piece of joint constructive thinking and deciding. The decision with which Mr. Lane suddenly faced them was obviously a very important one, and one which would affect not only their own lives but the lives of all the other boys and girls who were to come into the new house when it was built. It was this which brought to birth a community spirit of unusual vitality, which spent itself mainly in progressive growth and only secondarily in prohibitions. The building up of the community became the main focus for the impulses and for the conscious thought of the boys and girls—questions of conduct sank into their right place in a larger and broader whole.

Later experience has proved to me that the provision of the right kind of opportunity for the exercise of concerted thought and action is of the very first importance in the development of self-government.

Expect, for example, a group of factory youngsters to start governing themselves in club room or canteen through the necessity for some-one to regulate disorder, and probably internal jealousies will only still further disintegrate them. Give them a chance of having a social entertain-ment at which the comfort and enjoyment of their guests, mothers and baby brothers depends on their co-operation, and the whole crowd will combine together in the most unselfish way and will go forward from that moment.

Another most important element in the develop-ment of self-government at Flowers Farm was that Mr. Lane was one of the little group of boys and girls; he was not there as an authority, but as one of themselves. All ate at the same table, did the same work, sat at the same hearth, enjoyed the same laughs and shared each other's opinions. The thoughts of the grown-up helper at the Commonwealth were as much respected as those of the boys and girls. They were respected, not as the opinion of authority *qua* authority, but as the views of someone who had more experience, or more knowledge, or more skill than the rest of the community. Occasionally, when the community was considering some special difficulty, Kenneth, the boy chairman, with a thoughtful face and in slow tones as of an equal addressing an equal,

would say : " What does Mr. Lane think about
it ? " or (very occasionally) : " What does Miss
Bazeley think about it ? " H.M.I. the late Mr.
Charles Russell [1] said that the bearing of our boys
and girls was like that of undergraduates. I
think that it was in the relationship between the
boys and girls and the helpers or visitors that we
touched the university spirit most nearly ; it was
the kind of thing that is met with in the best
relationship between senior and junior common
room. The prestige of the grown-up was not
that of a member of staff, nor of a member of the

---

[1] H.M.I. Mr. Russell (the Chief Inspector of Home Office Schools)
visited us in January 1917. On his way from the station he told Mr.
Lane that he was sure he should not like the Commonwealth and that
it would be impossible to certify it for grant as a Home Office school.
Mr. Lane replied that he was greatly relieved to hear this, as he was
himself convinced that it was impossible to run the Commonwealth
in such a way as to win Home Office approval and grants. After this
beginning it was extremely interesting to observe the effect produced
on Mr. Russell by his short stay at the Commonwealth. He went
about freely among the boys and girls, chatting to them at their work
or in the family sitting-rooms. Next day he told Mr. Lane that he
had changed his mind, that he should recommend that the Commonwealth should be certified as a Reformatory school so that it might
receive the maximum grant under the Home Office, and that he wished
we could, in addition, become a training school for reformatory workers.
Mr. Lane replied that he would very much rather the Commonwealth did not become a Home Office school, that if we received a
Home Office grant we should be expected to conform to Home Office
ways and that it would be impossible to run the Commonwealth on
those lines. Mr. Russell replied that the Home Office would give
him an absolutely free hand to run the Commonwealth as he thought
best. Mr. Russell left us in the most cordial manner. Mr. Lane
returned from the station silent and depressed. He was, however,
reassured by receiving a letter from H.M.I. a few days later confirming
the statement that he would be in no way hampered by Home Office
regulations and that he would be given an entirely free hand. Not
long afterwards we received the sad news of the death of Mr. Russell,
and one cannot help wondering whether, if Mr. Russell had remained
at the Home Office, the subsequent history of the Commonwealth
might not have been different.

committee, nor of a member of the House of Lords, but the enormous prestige of a man of understanding and skill among a band of intelligent and sensitive youngsters. The prestige of an unassuming master-builder among really keen apprentices. The Lord Sandwich who found a wheelbarrow and took it round the grounds collecting all the old tin cans he could find enjoyed a totally different position from the Lord Sandwich who, on his first arrival, was addressed as " O Lord " by a flurried citizen possessing a dim remembrance of the Prayer-book. Long after, an unfortunate boy of good family who failed to scrub his landing, explained to the meeting that he was a gentleman and need not work, and was firmly reminded that Lord Sandwich worked and *he* was a gentleman.

In spite of all my subsequent experience of committee meetings, I have never felt so much respect for my own opinion as when it was sought for by a quiet, steady, thoughtful citizen-chairman.

The boys and girls were thus not forced back upon themselves to grapple as best they might with communal difficulties. There was no shifting of all the responsibility on to the citizens ; the grown-up helpers did not lead a separate life whilst the boys and girls managed their own affairs. We were all citizens. All shared responsibilities, liabilities, ups and downs. If citizens ran away and had to be fetched back by train from distant towns, taxes were paid by everyone, helpers paying in silver and other citizens paying in aluminium. If a family fell on bad times and there was nothing in the house, all alike went without until some arrangement could be made. If rigorous limitation of household expenses was necessary in order to adjust the weekly quota to the earnings of the least efficient members of the family, all alike lived for a time on bread, onions and tea. Now and again a family had to choose between the expense of an extra house-girl to help the house-mother keep the house up to a higher standard and the expense of having margarine or syrup throughout the week with its bread; sometimes the choice would go one way and sometimes another. A family was normal and prosperous when earnings warranted a budget which included a sufficient number of house-girls and also meat on Sunday, and cheese, parkin, corn cake, Boston beans, blue peas, plenty of garden vegetables, and cocoa as well as tea during the week.

The Family

The family was one of the most powerful of all the forces in the Commonwealth. The family made you; your failures could undo the family. On first arriving, a citizen was adopted into which-ever family had a spare place. The greater part of the time there were two families, Bramble and

Veronica. Bracken house had been burnt down, but had been rebuilt and was waiting to be occupied in 1916. Heather was the smallest of the houses, and in 1916 was used as the hostel for visitors, and later, when the little ones were becoming too big to find room enough in the citizens' houses, Heather was taken over by Mrs. Lane and made into the little ones' home.

About eighteen boys and girls formed one family, together with the house-mother and one or two grown-up helpers. At one end of the house was the staircase to the boys' landing, at the other end the staircase to the girls' landing. Neither the boys nor the girls went on to each others' landings. The boys had to scrub their own floors and keep their own rooms and baths in order and make their own beds. Belowstairs was the family dining-room, family sitting-room, one or two helpers' rooms, besides the kitchen, larder, etc.

There were thus, within the Commonwealth, two circles of intimates who, by living together, trusted each other, had experienced each other's strong and weak points, and knew each other well enough to act and speak freely and spontaneously. I think that the vitality of the community life and of public opinion and its genuinely democratic spirit was very largely due to the existence within the Commonwealth of these two circles of intimates of different ages, temperaments, and of very different intellectual resources, who were in the habit of exchanging views freely at the family meal or fireside. But what we needed in 1916 was, not two such circles, but permission to start four or five. ⟶

I was amazed, when I first went to the Commonwealth, at the outspokenness of the community meetings. No one was afraid to be himself, no one was afraid to give himself away. You could criticize another in the most direct and searching manner, or you could say or do the kindest thing possible for another. Often in other self-governing institutions one finds that the government is inclined to be weak and lethargic, because it is not backed up by, nor expressed by, a sensitive and articulate public opinion. But at the Commonwealth public opinion was quick, vigorous and sensitive. It was interesting to observe that sometimes public opinion, the community mind, was in advance of the opinion of prominent individuals, and sometimes it lagged quite behind the intuitions of the most thoughtful boy or girl.

This vitality of the community mind was due to the character of the families. In these there was no approach to the autocratic or patriarchal families of the outside world. Too often, in the outside world, the family is a weakness to society rather than a strength. The elders dominate the younger members; the elders want to act providence to all their dependents and, worse still, the family endeavours to keep all its younger members safely within the family circle, so that the ideal of living with and for one's generation is sacrificed upon the altar of caring for one's family.

But the Commonwealth family was co-operative and not patriarchal. It was a resting-place for its members after work in the bigger community; it was a place where they might get refreshment or home-truths, as the case might be. It was a landing-place to which they might return or from which they might start off on fresh efforts or fresh facings of reality.

The family protected its weaklings or spurred them on to effort if it thought they were shirking. The family approved of you or criticized your dress and manners. The family combined in its large heart the sometimes conflicting impulses of loyalty to its members and loyalty to the maintenance of community standards of ethics and conduct. It provided its members with many opportunities for service and for the most delightfully sensitive and unpretentious good manners.

Later, when Mr. Lane's unconventionality in sharing the simplicity and homeliness of citizen family life was questioned by the Home Office, Margaret, the simplest and most gifted of our house-mothers, commented to me on the views of these eminent authorities. " I can't understand them, Miss Bazeley; seems as if they don't know what Daddy's made of; they don't seem to know that men and women are all alike. Seems as if they had never lived in a family."

The family meals were the daily informal occasions when all the members of a family gathered together. They might be passed almost in silence, or in desultory conversation. They might be made an occasion for warfare between Annie and Carrie, who never could live peaceably together for long, which would be abruptly broken off in a combined attempt to make Jane mend her table manners (the family finally sent Jane, who was a very backward child, to have a course of breakfasts with me at Heather in order that she might have some tuition in table manners). Now and again, especially at supper, or at tea-time on Sunday, when there was a feeling of leisure, a discussion would spring up casually, the talk would become more and more interesting, and citizens from another house would drift in and remain to listen.

Meals were sometimes a delightful social function. I remember a birthday tea for Raymond Lane [1] at which his younger brother was chosen to present him with a large bouquet, composed of all the flowers in the Commonwealth. I remember a welcome-home tea for Mr. Lane and the girls when they returned from Torquay after the crisis in 1917, and later in that autumn a birthday tea

[1] Mr. Lane's children spent all their holidays at the Commonwealth, sharing as citizens in the life and work of the place. Raymond, who was at Sherborne School, was often with us ; we could not have done without his help on the farm, and he took a leading part as a citizen. The youngest boy was an ardent farmer and did not go away to school.

for Mr. Lane, at which he made a delightful little speech.

These functions were generally preceded by hours of scurrying and shouting. The house was scrubbed from top to toe. The boys brought in mare's-tails from the swamp and trailing things and flowers from the coppice to decorate the tables and the dining-room. The house-mother and I spent a feverish morning making custard moulds and cakes. On the occasion of the return from Torquay, Annie was temporary house-mother at Bramble and got into trouble because she allowed her protégé, Fred, a shiftless younger boy, who was on close bounds, but who happened to be the best writer in the Commonwealth, to print the placard of welcome and put it up over the front door. Finally, all would be ready, and the great moment would arrive when the family and guests would gather round the tea-tables. Very little would be eaten, in spite of Annie's or Margaret's hospitable pressure, but all would be very happy and at peace with one another.

During the winter of 1916–17 we had many delightful evening meals at Heather. I have described elsewhere how the law of compulsory education was amended in the autumn of 1916. After this about ten girls desired to have cooking lessons. I divided them into pairs, and each pair took one or more evenings a week. The pair would arrive in the afternoon and prepare a meal for eight or ten people (including themselves, the house-girl and myself).   Louie, the house-girl, took great pains polishing her table and her cutlery and preparing as pleasant a room and supper-table as possible.   The cooks acted as hostesses and invited three or four boys and girls as guests.   Mr. Lane was invariably invited.   It was always a friendly and happy party which assembled in the pleasant Heather common room.   Louie took a delight in her pretty table and brightly burning lamp (something of an achievement for a Commonwealth lamp).   The hostesses were surprised and pleased at the success of their efforts in the kitchen, which reached a level far above anything previously attained in the family kitchens.   The guests were refreshed with the change of not being at home and of eating slightly different food in different surroundings.   All were deeply interested in the conversation.   Mr. Lane deftly led it on to topics which would interest the citizens and by which, though they were unaware of it, he had often some contribution to make, by way of comment, suggestion or contrast, to the thoughts and events which happened to be occupying the citizens' minds at that particular time.

One evening we had an account of his boyhood, when he had run away from home to live with the Ojibway Indians ; he gave us a description of the play of the Indian boys and girls and of their code of conduct and manners.   Other topics were a

Cuban tornado, ice-floes and the *Titanic* disaster, the play of wild animals, days at the Ford Republic. Among the latter was a description of a fire and the work of rescuing the boys; he himself had become almost helpless in the effort to rescue one of the boys, when Mrs. Lane's voice reached him through the smoke and dragged him back from unconsciousness, and he was able to get the boy out.

I remember an account of life on a sugar plantation and of how, as a small boy, he saw sugar being made. There was a description also of a Western lumber-camp and of some of his friends among his fellow-lumbermen, and of how they were the most genuinely religious-natured men he knew. He told us, too, of the Swami Vivikenanda, whom he had known in America, and of his wonderful teaching about prayer and work.

There was, I remember, an occasion when Margaret and Jessie were the cooks and Mr. Lane, Mr. Poole (the old carpenter) and Carrie were the guests, Louie and Irene the house-girls. It was a November evening and we were sitting round our log fire afterwards. The talk was about the ice palaces of Quebec and the extravagance of life in New York. Suddenly Carrie, who resented what she called religion, plunged into a question about religion. Margaret answered: " Mr. Lane's religion is to be happy, Miss Bazeley's is to be happy, Mr. Poole's is his work, Irene's is to smile, mine— I shan't tell you what mine is. Do you believe in saying your prayers, Daddy, when you get up and go to bed?" Mr. Lane: "I believe in saying them all day and all the time."

On other occasions the boys would enjoy table games—the girls did not care about these so much. Above all, we had a Novlart stencilling outfit, and the boys who could make a sustained effort surprised themselves producing fascinating pictures of moonlit landscapes and seascapes.

Early in 1917 we had several cases of influenza, and Heather dining-room was turned into a hospital ward. We did not have many more cookery lessons and supper-parties after that, as the spring came and every hand had to turn to planting potatoes and to other labours in the garden and on the farm. Mrs. Lane and I sat for many hours on the sheltered side of the courtyard cutting great piles of potatoes into eyes for planting. Meanwhile Mr. Lane and some boys were ploughing certain fields into potato furrows. The weather was fine and dry and the house-girls, with some of the little ones from Heather, together with Mrs. Lane and myself, planted the potatoes in the furrows. The little ones were the most expert. They ran nimbly along the furrows and dropped the potatoes at equal distances into them. We others had to go more laboriously, measuring with a stick the distances prescribed for us, as we found in time, after fatigue began to set in, that we quite miscalculated our distances, and unequal spacing would have greatly increased the labour of the subsequent processes of cultivation.

For my first four or five months at the Commonwealth I lived at Heather Cottage, the hostel for visitors and practising-kitchen for girl citizens. A member of the adult staff left early in 1917 and it became necessary to rearrange the houses. Mrs. Lane and the nine little ones, now grown rather too big to find comfortable quarters in the small amount of space which could be given them by Veronica family, went to find their home in Heather, and I went to live as helper at Bramble. After about nine months another member of the staff, Mrs. Lewis, left the Commonwealth with her daughter Doreen, and I went to live at Veronica as house-mother. I thus had opportunities of seeing the Commonwealth from every possible point of view. Whilst I was at Heather and unattached to a family, I used often to spend an hour or so in the evening in Mr. Lane's sitting-room with the Bramble girls, and I thus got an inside view of a Commonwealth family. After I became a helper living with the Bramble family, my point of observation changed, as my room then became " the home " for the Bramble boys. Later again, when I was at Veronica, my room became the sitting-room for a permutation of Veronica boys. Thus I was fortunate in having opportunities for observing Commonwealth family life from three different angles, each family and each group within the family having a very distinct individuality of its own. It was noticeable that meals were the chief occasions when the family of boys and girls met together. During the rest of their leisure time there was a marked tendency for girls to seek the company of girls and boys of boys. The girls adopted Mr. Lane's sitting-room as their evening " home," the boys Mrs. Lane's or mine. Not always the same boys or the same girls would form these groups, but there would be a steady nucleus with a fluctuating fringe.

We never attempted to entertain one another in these sitting-room groups ; we were just a circle of friends gathered round the same lamp and fire. Mr. Lane used to sit at his desk writing, or in his arm-chair reading or thinking and, of course, smoking, whilst the citizens were engaged in various distracting pursuits about the room. Ethel and Jessie might be dictating shorthand to one another (they had joined a business correspondence school). Carrie might be reading detective stories, Annie playing the gramophone. Mr. Lane believed that the citizens needed to have their leisure unorganized. The days were fairly strenuous ; the pressure of working seriously at any of the Commonwealth trades forced an organization upon the citizens which, with their tendency towards short-spanned attention, they found sufficiently exacting. Two evenings in the week were taken up with the community meetings, and the rest of the evenings the citizens did not seem to need to have planned out into definite occupations beforehand. Some of the citizens read a fair amount, boys rather more than girls. If a boy read, he read Graham White on " Aviation " or Curwood or Seton Thompson's animal stories. If a girl read, she sought a detective story or other thriller. The novel was not sought for. A great many of the citizens never read (one or two were illiterate, whilst others could do advanced work), but nearly all liked to decorate their rooms with a selection of brightly bound books. Books would disappear out of the library and would reappear in a neat row on a citizen's shelf. A complaint would be brought into court every now and again against a citizen for spoiling a book ; this always roused the wrath of the community and a fine would be inflicted. At one period a boy and girl (Leonard and Jessie) were asked to reorganize the library and to draw up a set of rules which would work, and report to the next meeting ; they were not ready in a week, but in a fortnight they produced a scheme of rules which I remember thinking were excellent, though I do not now recollect what they were. As one who has groaned under the failings of normal students in the matter of books, I felt that our delinquents had a high standard of morals where the library was concerned.

The following extracts from my diary illustrate one or two of the evening groups.

Tuesday, January 16th.—I spent part of the evening sitting in H. L.'s room with Annie, Susan and some of the other girls, putting up and choosing pictures, prints from my portfolio of trees. Presently they were shrieking and laughing over some Bairnsfather drawings. H. L. says this always happens, it is their unconscious reaction against something they do not understand.

Wednesday, January 17th.—Sat in H. L.'s room with the girls for a little while before the meeting. We fell to talking about God. Carrie said she did not believe much in God, " Not all the time." Margaret : " Then you can't believe at all." Carrie : " Well, I don't, then." It started from spirit-healing. Carrie : " I don't believe in angels and spirits." Margaret : " Well, God is a Spirit."

Tuesday, January 30th.—The pump is broken, there is no water at the hostel, and a short allowance in the other houses. Evening, sat in H. L.'s room with the girls. Annie beginning to talk more (quite nicely) and rougher than usual, in boy's boots and overalls (she had lately taken on garden work). She cuffed Jane several times in a friendly, if aggravating, way, " because I feel like it." We looked at patterns of chintzes and cretonnes and chose one for H. L.'s arm-chair. H. L. has had to answer a county court summons for going to Torquay without notifying the police. King's attorney said it was a very serious offence, but it was dismissed with costs, 4s. Gramophone playing at all times, but Carrie puts it off when H. L. wants to talk. She has it on all the time she is doing his rooms in the morning. Mrs. Edwards was knocked over by the ram and hurt her ankle. The farm boys, having stood in the courtyard for two days,[1] came and asked to have their work back.

[1] If a citizen quitted his job, or was dismissed by his foreman, and if he failed to find fresh work, he had to stand in the courtyard during working hours.

Wednesday, January 31*st.*—Education of Jane occupies the girls much. In the evening sat in H. L.'s room with the girls. Jane began to cry, and Carrie to console her, because she did not like to see her cry, and Annie to upbraid Carrie because it was spoiling Jane. They are a mixture of exactingness and kindness, which is very effective. H. L. gave us a very exciting account of the poor whites of Kentucky, but Carrie went on with her book. Jessie and Annie very much interested, especially Jessie ; Kentucky, because the gramophone plays, " It's a long way to my home in Kentucky," and Jessie asked, " Where is Kentucky ? "

Friday, February 2*nd.*—Inspected all the houses and glory-holes. Mrs. Lane and I enjoyed looking at some patterns of hand-weaving. H. L. hauling coal and hay and just escaped killing ; the lorry skidded and he let go just in time to be thrown over the hedge into the field instead of being pinned underneath. He fell on his head and shoulders and was dazed for a few minutes. He spent the rest of the afternoon hauling timber as usual. Sat with the girls in his sitting-room before the court. Carrie reduced to giggles and jokes about the mortuary (where she went to identify her mother), and said laughingly, " If Daddy had been killed, we should all have had to go to the mortuary to identify him." Annie and Jessie disapproved. The latter : " Well, how should we be able to get on without Daddy ? " Fetched water from the well by moonlight with Jessie, as the pump is out of order. Mended sewing-machine with Annie.

Saturday, February 3*rd.*—Jane sitting in H. L.'s sitting-room in the evening with an illustrated children's Bible story-book with very conventional illustrations. She began tearing out the coloured pictures and shoving them at Carrie, on whom she is at present chiefly dependent. Carrie, Louie and Jane all began looking at the pictures. Ethel, calmly and distantly : " It's all lies." The other three said they were lovely.

Sunday, February 4*th.*—Kenneth, George, Allan [1] and

---

[1] Allan was the youngest Lane.

Jessie to tea. Talked about New Zealand and the chance of becoming a student citizen. Kenneth thought it a good chance and meant to take it. George knew he shouldn't stick to it, and so wasn't going to begin. We did stencil pictures, which one of our friends had sent us, with very great interest. Allan left off first, then George. Kenneth stayed till 9.0 absorbed in it. At first he did it slowly, then with more and more power. He tidied up before he went, the others just left their things lying about.

Thursday, February 8th.—After supper H. L. spent a little while cutting out the chair cover. Carrie and Allan ragging the whole time. Carrie (aged 17) is about the same mental age as Allan (aged 9). Annie dancing to the gramophone and taking off all the others; she did it very well till she got tired and went to sleep by the fire, and woke to call Florence a damned fool for looking at her. When H. L. objected, she subsided. Jessie and Ethel dictating shorthand to one another continuously through all the racket.

Thursday, February 15th.—Sat in H. L.'s room with the girls for a bit, whilst the vicar held a confirmation class in my room at Heather. I began making a dress for one of the little ones; Mr. Lane, Carrie and Jessie were deep in their books. Annie was much worried because no one would talk, nor even have the gramophone. Finally she settled down, satisfied with some comic papers. Her (step-) mother sends her a bundle every now and again. This time she had sixteen; as Mr. Lane pointed out the humour in them is all based on making someone who is in a superior position uncomfortable, e.g. the policeman is outwitted by the crook, the toff slips up on a piece of orange-peel.

In the spring of 1917, Bramble family was having a very uncomfortable time owing to the quarrels of the older girls; three boys (including John) left the family and applied for vacant places at Veronica. The next evening we had a house meeting after supper. Mr. Lane said that as it was useless to try to carry on a family in a house where the girls could not live peaceably together, we should become a " committee house " and have our lives ordered for us ; we should do exactly what he, as Superintendent, told us to do ; and he would distribute us for our meals among the other houses. The girls were still quarrelling. In the middle Annie called upon Jane to eat more quietly, and we all laughed and then wished our Superintendent " Good night, sir ! " The next day we had our last meals in Bramble ; we were quite a peaceful, happy family, and there was some quiet lamentation over how horrid it was to have the family broken up and to have to go and live with the neighbours ; Mr. Lane disliked it as much as the rest. Two or three days later Mr. Lane told me he was putting a notice on the bulletin board inviting citizens to join the Bramble Workers' Club. He looked in before breakfast to show me the notice he was about to put up, and which was as follows :

NOTICE.

On Saturday Bramble Cottage will be occupied by the Workers' Club. The Club will have as its objects :

1. To bring together in family life those who—

    (*a*) Enjoy work and take pride in a job well and quickly done.

(*b*) Feel that they can not only do their own job well, but who will be able to help others enjoy their work.

(*c*) Enjoy life better surrounded by happy, cheerful people.

(*d*) Like good, clean fun, and are not annoyed by any noise that is not vulgar or unkind.

(*e*) Are unhappy when another is hurt.

(*f*) Dislike prigs.

(*g*) Wish to see the Commonwealth take the place of reformatories.

(*h*) Like clean, well-cooked, appetizing food.

(*i*) Are willing to abide by the decision of the majority.

The Club will begin with one member who will choose from any who apply for membership another member, these two will choose a third, the three a fourth, and so on until the house is filled to its fullest capacity.

"Dining-Room Members" may be elected after all the rooms are occupied, if any such apply. One vote against an applicant will bar his or her membership.

Dues will be 13s. a week, including house-rent.

Dining-Room Members, 12s.

There will be no House-mother and no servants. The work of the house will be done by members of the family in rotation voluntarily, until there are sufficient members to employ a housekeeper at 16s. a week.

Members will be instructed in cookery and house-work when their turn comes, if they request it.

Applications in writing to Mr. Lane.

N.B.—Those who never make any mistakes

NEED NOT APPLY.

Mr. Lane invited me to make the first application. Having replied that I should be proud to do so, I was declared elected unanimously. Later in the day we had the first meeting of the Club. He and I elected Florence, then the three of us Jessie, then the four Carrie. This was followed by a long debate over Annie; she was finally elected and was followed by Leonard.

The next morning Bramble Workers' Club had its first breakfast. We were all very thankful to be gathered together again in our own home. We elected Edmund and rejected Gertrude and Miriam; Gertrude, because " we feel we cannot help Gertrude as much as Mary can " (in whose charge she was at Heather house), and Miriam because she had already withdrawn her application because Gertrude had applied.

The Club flourished for a time but, after many vicissitudes, it faded away, and Bramble reappeared as a family.

CHAPTER III

EDUCATIONAL FORCES—*continued*

WORK AND WAGES. A NOTE ON CITIZENS AND
THEIR HOMES

THE WORK

THE work at the Little Commonwealth fell into
two spheres, the boys' and the girls', and there
was no overlapping between the two.

For the girls there were the houses, the garden,
the laundry and the shop. Two or three house-
girls, or none at all, according to its means, would
be employed by a family to work under the direction of the citizen house-mother. The very large
and productive garden was in the charge of the
head garden girl and was entirely worked by girls.
The field out of which it had been formed had
originally been ploughed and fenced by the boys,
but from that point the girls took it over and
worked it very successfully. The garden provided
a large part of our food; the amount of meat
imported into the Commonwealth was reduced to
a minimum during the last eighteen months and
we lived very largely on vegetables. We also
counted on the garden for a certain amount of
money income. Our onion crops were quite

valuable in the later war period. But, as in other Commonwealth ventures, no counting definitely on one's harvest was possible ; a day or two's carelessness, and the most hopeful prospects might be destroyed.

The laundry manageress was a girl citizen ; she employed other girls to work on the calender and do the ironing and folding. The machinery was all modern and steam-driven, and the engine, in charge of the boy engineer and stoker, was in a quite separate engine-room. There was always a grown-up helper working in the laundry. Mr. Lane did the heavy lifting and packing of clothes from one machine into another, Mrs. Lane or I worked with the others at the decoudon or ironing.

The shop was generally in charge of a girl shopkeeper, but occasionally of a boy. The shopkeeper employed others to help her keep the shop and store-rooms clean and sorted. She kept the accounts and delivered the weekly bills to the families.

The families paid their bills in aluminium currency, in which the citizens' wages had been paid. If a citizen needed personal things, clothes or boots or perhaps a folding foot-rule or a tie, he needed to have earned a large enough weekly wage to have a margin over after paying his share of the family bill. He could then put an order into the shop, and what he needed was procured the next time anyone went to Sherborne. His aluminium money had the same purchasing power in the shop that the equivalent silver coins would have had outside. But it was only the more stable citizens who ever had this margin. Quite often a shiftless citizen who could not keep his job would have no money for new clothes or boots. The more shiftless a citizen the more careless he or she seemed to be of his clothes and, in spite of having been respectably clothed to start with, by friends outside, he would soon be going about in rags. This would be more than the family could stand, and certain additions to the wardrobe would be ordered at the family expense. The realization that other members of his family were clothing him sometimes became the first incentive towards steady work.

The boys had rather more range in their work than the girls. There was the farm, with all its different departments; the cows and the dairy, with milking and butter-making; the care of the pigs, the calves and the sheep; the horses and the carting work; the ploughing, sowing, harvesting and rick-building; the hedging and ditching. There was also timber-felling and hauling. The engineer's department had charge of the engine which pumped the water to the different houses; of the laundry engine, which, in addition, was made to drive the circular saw; of the motors and of the lorry which hauled coal, and also, after

Mr. Lane and the boys had transformed its wheels, served as farm tractor in the fields.

The building and carpentering department generally had some work in hand. The houses were finished by 1916, but there were still new farm stables to be built and a dairy and a calf-house to be reconstructed out of a part of the original farm buildings.

In all these different departments wages were paid in a Commonwealth aluminium currency. A boy or girl foreman would make out the time-sheets and would dock an employé's wages for carelessness or unpunctuality. Out of his wages a citizen paid his share of the family bills and bought his clothes from the shop and any additional things for which he had the money. If he went home for a holiday, and owed no money anywhere in the Commonwealth, any balance he might have could be changed in the office from aluminium into English money. Economic necessity, the fact that if a man would eat he must also work, was at the basis of our self-government. I do not think that, without it, a crowd of lawless young delinquents, each with (to start with) egocentric and individualistic ideals, could have developed into a good society. No one could escape from the impersonal impact of cause and effect in the economic necessity which beset him. Necessity pressed itself home as a purpose on each individual every day—a purpose which compelled you to face it and yourself and to take up the challenge of life. What made this challenge of necessity one from which it was impossible to escape? It was because every day demonstrated the truth, not in words, but with the incontrovertible argument of event, that the life of the individual is inseparably bound up with that of the family and of the community, and that no one can live to himself without weakening society.

The working life of the Commonwealth approached that of a frontier farm. It was many sided, it was interesting, exhausting and never done. We were almost, but not quite, self-contained, and had to do for ourselves in as many ways as possible. Every citizen thus had the opportunity of gaining all-round resource and *savoir-faire* as well as more expert knowledge. Some of the boy engineers have gone on to do very well with big engineering firms. Leonard, at one time in charge of the dairy, went to an agricultural college later and thence to Canada. Jessie went for a time on to a chicken farm. If we had had more money, we should have admitted more citizens and extended our plant. We could then, in addition to building our own houses, have baked our own bread and made our own clothes. But education by doing, with pupils of the Commonwealth type, is expensive. They are very heavy on tools and materials of every description. It is only education by words that is cheap, and we consequently had to limit both the numbers of our population and the variety of trades we could teach them. It would have been interesting to introduce weaving and dyeing—I am a believer in the virtues of handling colour—also cabinet-making and metal-work for the boys and carpentry for the girls. In addition to building houses we might have studied the development of the house and of architecture. But though we were unable deliberately to introduce the cultural and artistic element of these crafts, the Commonwealth buildings themselves were singularly pleasant to look upon. They were harmoniously proportioned and grouped. Their structure and material were satisfying, and fitted in perfectly with the Dorsetshire country-side. Our courtyard, with the little round-headed arch into the garden at one corner, was a friendly place, speaking of a pleasant life in common. Just as the round-arched brick-built fire-places helped to keep the families together, so the courtyard, with its low wall forming a pleasant seat round the sunk paved space in the middle, which had been made by Mr. Lane and the first boys, suggested an invitation to pause and enjoy shelter, hospitality and friendly intercourse.

On a former page I have made allusion to the fact that the citizens occasionally revisited their homes. Such visits were rare, but they were eagerly looked for. The citizens' whole-hearted loyalty to, and affection for, their homes, however wretched these might, in fact, be, together with their spells of home-sickness, were at first a surprising feature of their mentality, equalled only by the vigour and confidence of their return to the Commonwealth. Baffled by home circumstances, a girl such as Margaret, Louie or Susan might perhaps, for the first time, realize that she was powerless to help for good in the chaos of a drunken or dissolute home, and she would return to the Commonwealth with a new perspective, a deeper insight, and a radiant power to help in the affairs of the Commonwealth. Or a boy such as Leonard, from a good home, would return full of healthy hopes and intentions, with the future opening out before him, because his family had appreciated him and the changes which had taken place in him since he had come to the Commonwealth.

Margaret was one of the original trio of citizens, the leader of the gang of little girls referred to on page 33, who had eluded the police and stolen successfully for weeks from the open stalls in the street-markets round their home. She was a girl of a most lovable, sympathetic and sensible disposition, a born mother, friend and house-mother. Her parents were unsuccessful coster folk. In their early married life they had put all their money into buying mementoes to sell at the Derby. That particular Derby Day was a deluge, they could not sell their perishable merchandise, and their fortunes never recovered from the early blow. They sought comfort in the public-house more and more, and Margaret and her younger brother and sister grew up in the deprivation, uncertainty and violence of a drunken home.

Two or three months after Margaret had been in the Commonwealth she became home-sick, and at last Mr. Lane told her that he was going up to London the next day and if she liked she might go home with him. Before parting from her, Mr. Lane gave her his London address and told her when he was returning to the Commonwealth. The day of his return a message came from Margaret, " Do come." He went down to Poplar. Margaret ran out to meet him and whispered, " I want to come back. I love mother, but somehow it's not the same. I wish she would wash her hair." Unconsciously Margaret's standard had been raised since she had been a child at home, and her love was to develop with her change of standard. Mr. Lane went into the house to have a chat with her father and mother, and they offered him the biggest courtesy they could, genuine hospitality and the sharing of their cup of tea. Mr. Lane drank his out of the lid of the teapot, because the other two cups were too badly cracked to be offered to a guest.

Margaret returned to the Commonwealth, but some six months later she again asked to go home.

" But," said Mr. Lane, " last time you weren't happy, and you will find things rather worse this time." " Yes," said Margaret. " But it doesn't seem right for me to be here having all these lovely things and for mother to be there having nothing. I might be able to help mother." " Yes," said Mr. Lane. " But don't you think you would be able to help her more later on, if you stayed here and learnt all you could? " Margaret thought it over, and stayed. Later, as a young woman, she gave up her post as house-mother and went home. This was partly due to a fit of restlessness and partly because she was uneasy about her little brother and wanted to take care of him. After an interval of six months or so we were plunged into our Home Office diffi-culties. Margaret heard of this and, realizing how our life was suffering from the constant interruptions and from inadequate house-mothers, she returned and took up her old post as house-mother and did extraordinarily well, helping to keep things going right up to the very end.

I add a letter belonging to this latter period.

LITTLE COMMONWEALTH,
BATSCOMBE.

MY DEAR MISS BASLEY,
Thanks very very much for your nice letter it is so nice to hear from you and to know what you are doing. when are you coming to see us agane do come soon it is nice to have the People who Love the L.C. to come back to it,

Yes my stove is going on fine i am glad to say. The
Family are doing well a little trouble now and again, Ethel
lost her job agane yesterday and got it back this morning
a lot of babys,

Daddy look as tho he could do with a few weeks holiday
I wish he would go away. We are having a lot of stealing
going on but cant find out who it is. Tom —— is staying
with us and he looks well. Wouldent I love to be with you
and go into the woods it must be Peaceful. Bramble
smash up agane as usual, it is enough to drive daddy in his
grave it wont belong if things keep going on as they are
know. its almost time for B Poast so must close will write
you more soon. do let me know all you are doing.

Your Friend
MARGARET.

Just been inspecting boys Rooms or Pig stys.

Leonard came from a totally different type of
home. His people were comfortably situated in
an official position. I should judge that the home
was educated and refined. He had a young
stepmother and little stepsisters. His stepmother
was particularly kind and perhaps over-anxious to
take care of him. He was a fine, well-grown lad,
very big for his age when he started stealing, at
first from his father's pockets, later, to his parents'
horror, from the missionary boxes at Sunday-
school. They begged Mr. Lane to take him at
the Commonwealth, and the Commonwealth seemed
to be exactly what he needed to straighten out.
There was no more stealing. He had a few quite
minor faults of forgetfulness or slowness, which
any boy might have, but it seemed that the impulse

to steal had been an impulse to obtain power; the big, intelligent boy had been, in his over-careful home, treated too much as a child (as, indeed, he was in years). At the Commonwealth, constructive work and the community life gave him the independence and power which he needed for his proper development. No wonder his mother wrote a delighted letter to Mr. Lane after Leonard's first visit home, expressing his parents' surprise when they saw what a fine lad he was becoming.

Philip was one of our boys who enlisted. He left in a hurry, and his reputation was a little clouded because of the undischarged debt he had left behind him in the shop. On his first leave from France he came straight back to the Commonwealth before going home. There was a well-poised, thoughtful, almost wistful look in his face, as he sat quietly talking to the citizens in Bramble porch. He stayed a day or two with us and then went home. Before leaving, he quietly paid off all that he owed in the shop, though the debt had been long ago forgotten by all the rest of us. He was killed later in France.

CHAPTER IV

OTHER EDUCATIONAL FORCES

THE COMMUNITY. OFFICES. THE SCHOOL. CHURCH

DAILY and hourly we met life as members of a family. But we also belonged to a larger unit, namely, the community. I have had considerable experience of associations of young people, but I have never come across one where the community spirit was so strong. It looked at you from the eyes of every citizen, it met you in innumerable ways throughout the day. The community met twice a week to consider its affairs and take action where necessary. Once a week the court was held, and on the other evening, the legislative meeting; both assemblies were presided over by a citizen. It was considered an insult to the community not to attend a meeting. I came to see that these meetings were of the utmost importance in the re-education of the citizens. They gave opportunities for genuine bits of co-operative thinking. The process might be slow, it might be groping, or it might show a swift intuition for going straight to the essentials of a situation. In the meetings we had a mirror in which the affairs of the community were reflected, in which everyone could get a glimpse of what he or she really looked like. During the meeting, the community focused its mind on the happenings of life; it gave us an opportunity for an examination and a criticism of life, for a facing of difficulties and of tendencies and for a digging out of principles. A meeting was, in fact, an occasion for searching group analysis (though the citizens were quite unconscious of the fact), and its effectiveness as a school for thought and character was due partly to the mutual confidence between all members of the community, and partly to our primal assumption, which no one ever questioned, that every one genuinely and seriously cared, each in his degree, for the good of the community and of the individual. I have never lived in a more socialized community, nor one in which individuality was more marked.

The meeting was attended, as I have said, by all citizens. We had with us, from time to time, a boy or a girl who was not yet of an age for citizenship. The normal age for citizenship was fourteen. Mr. Lane did not believe that self-government of our complete and searching quality was suitable for younger children. At adolescence the impulse of disinterested loyalty to a group or to ideals makes itself felt normally for the first time. Younger children certainly co-operate together, but generally for motives of self-interest. If one will not take one's turn at fielding, one cannot expect to take one's turn as batsman. If one will not take one's turn as squaw or faithful follower, one cannot hope, in turn, to play the rôle of Indian chief. Younger children need many hours of free and unsupervised play, set in a fairly stable framework organized by an intelligent, sympathetic, instructed and undominating authority. At adolescence the spirit of the child appears to be reborn at a deeper level. It begins to manifest itself in loyalty to a group, in the formulation of ideals, social or individual, and in a desire to act for oneself and to go with people of one's own age. A strain is often caused because the childish tendency to dependence is not yet exhausted (and may not be for many years), and comes into conflict at times with the increasing tendency towards a more grown-up self-determination. In some children psychical and spiritual adolescence sets in rather before the period of the physiological changes, and these children are ready at an earlier age for self-government. The reverse also happens sometimes, the development of spiritual adolescence being retarded until a long time after physiological growth has taken place.

We had all three stages of growth in our Commonwealth population. Leonard and Jessie had come to us before they were thirteen, and they asked for, and were given, their citizenship by the community before they reached the accepted age of fourteen; on the other hand was Ida, a fifteen-year-old girl, whose greatest friend was nine-year-old

Julia, and who was perfectly happy to be taken over into the schoolroom group and to do ordinary lessons with the little ones and ordinary play or gardening as a recreation in play hours. There were also Martha and two or three other boys and girls among the later comers who spent their time fluctuating between efforts at self-support and periods of failure, when they were supported by the family and handed over to the care and supervision of the house-mother or of another citizen.

Nomination of Citizen Officers

The method of nomination of officers of the community presented an interesting feature of commonwealth life. All offices were held for six months, and there were two main elections in the year. Every now and again a citizen would resign his office; or he might be impeached and at the next legislative meeting the chairman would ask if there were any nominations for the office. After a pause a boy or girl would stand up and say, "I nominate myself." This surprised me very much, until I realized that he was considered by everyone not to be assuming an honour or privilege, but to be offering himself to do some service for the community. The officer of the Public Works Department, for instance, had a quite exacting task. He kept the grounds tidy, he inspected the drains and the "glory-holes" of all the houses and the drains of the farm-yard. If a house-mother would not listen to his warning about grounds or glory-hole, it was his duty to bring a complaint against her at the next court. He also had to see that the assembly hall was ready for meetings, the fire lit and the lamp burning. He was empowered, on occasions, if he were in full-time employment himself, to employ a citizen to scrub the hall or tidy the grounds, and to bring in the bill to the community. Such casual jobs, under the Public Works Officer, were considered suitable for the weaker members of the community who could not yet keep continuous employment for any length of time and to whom the community were thankful to assign jobs which were within their capacity and which would help them to pay their way. Ginger, a rather disreputable small boy, was sometimes employed on these casual jobs by a helpful Public Works Officer, but the time came when the official for the time being was impeached and, to everyone's amazement, Ginger nominated himself for the office. Ginger had scarcely yet turned his own corner. His own room was habitually condemned for its condition at the daily inspection ; he could not keep any job, generally he did not seek one. He was usually allied with whoever happened at the moment to be passing through a thieving or absconding stage. The community, however, accepted Ginger's offer of service, and it never regretted doing so. For weeks—in fact, for so long that I lost count—he kept the grounds, the back yards and the farm-yard up to the mark; we never had looked so tidy, and Ginger himself became more respectable in the process. In general, we ebbed and flowed between tidiness and untidiness—a house might sink low; a complaint for untidiness would then be brought against the family, or its house-mother, in the weekly court. Failing that, the family might sink into a still more neglected state. The Superintendent might then step in and refuse, as representative of the committee, to employ anyone, boy or girl, from such a slum. With everyone out of work, family and industrial life was at a standstill. No meals could be served until the house was cleaned up, favourably reported upon, and the prospect in sight of the members being taken on again at their jobs. The citizens loved cleaning up; once at it, they threw themselves into it with the most whole-hearted zest. Every available inch would be scrubbed and scrubbed hard; everything possible would be polished—windows, tables, cupboards, stove. They knew exactly where all the dirty corners would be, and had them all out relentlessly. They went beyond the demands of utility and took an æsthetic pleasure in their doings; even the cocoa-tins would be polished and the dishes would appear in quite a different device on the dining-room shelves. In one of our untidy periods I remember asking Mr. Lane if we could not have an incinerator. The farm boys were getting slack about removing the dust-bins; then Major, the big dog, would come round and push off the lids and the kitchen refuse would be scattered all about, so that no place could be kept tidy. I wanted an incinerator to burn things at once, so that we might be untroubled by farm boys, dust-bins, or Major. Mr. Lane, however, replied to the effect that our occasional untidiness was one of the healthy symptoms of the Commonwealth, that it was only when disorder became apparent that we really fell to and took pains to deal with it; that the disorder of our grounds was closely linked with the disorder of our citizens' minds; and that the incinerator would do away with both the opportunity for bringing disorder to the surface and for exerting ourselves to deal with it when it was there. Visitors who came to us at these low-tide periods of disorder were occasionally shaken in their belief in Commonwealth methods in practical life. If they could have seen us at the other end too, at the high-water mark of order, they would have been reassured, if not surprised at the exactingness of the citizens' standard. Since then I too have had occasion to be amazed at the high standard of our boys and girls, even in their bad periods. The back yards and kitchen premises of some institutions for grown-ups, with responsible normal adult men and women employés, have scandalized me, and I have felt that never in our worst moments at the Little Commonwealth did we ever have anything so bad, nor should we have been indifferent to it if we had.

Other officers at the Little Commonwealth were the Boys' Court Commissioner and the Girls' Court Commissioner. These two had the onerous task of seeing that the boys and girls (if any) on " close bounds " were carrying out their penalties properly, e.g. going to bed at the prescribed hour, not talking or sitting in the family sitting-room. The two most important offices were those of Chairman of the Legislative and Judge of the Judicial Meeting. There were also the offices of Clerk and of Treasurer. It should be noted that in no case was the responsibility shifted from the community to the officer. In the case of the Public Works Department and the Court Commissioners, we had citizens offering to do the work of the community. If it were ill-done, they would be impeached and others nominated. The Judge and the Chairman were representatives of the community. Authority still rested in the community. The whole community was present at all meetings and either upheld the chair or, on occasions, challenged it.

Life at the Commonwealth sometimes required the same individual to assume two or three different rôles simultaneously; this demanded a certain agility of mind in turning from one thing to the next, or else a certain simplicity in taking things as they came. For example, Margaret, as Judge, at Friday evening's meeting sentenced Kendle, with great justice, to close bounds, for crookedness of behaviour. Kendle was one of the bigger lads, always dressed like a gentleman (not altogether from his own wardrobe), who, though admired for his appearance, was always rather disliked for his lack of straightness. On Saturday morning Margaret, as house-mother, was seeing Mr. Lane off in the Ford for Sherborne and giving him many commissions for her household, and added : " I wonder, Daddy, would it matter making Kendle a cake for his birthday, as he's on close bounds ? "

THE SCHOOL

The year before I went to the Commonwealth the citizens had passed a law of compulsory attendance at evening school. The teacher of the little ones kindly undertook to organize the school, and for a time things went fairly well. Then, as the winter drew out, the resources of the school became exhausted, and the evenings were apt to end in the piano and music, which led nowhere. The citizens, however, still kept the law of compulsory attendance, in spite of having lost interest in the school. They felt it was a disgrace to the Commonwealth to have an illiterate citizen. Such a one was Ginger, who had been brought up in a workhouse since his infancy and had not learnt to read or write. He had become more and more unmanageable at the workhouse and, having threatened the matron with a knife, was transferred to us.

Mr. Lane was more disappointed than the citizens at the failure of the school to interest them or lead them anywhere. The citizens were conservative enough to expect to be bored in school and to think that attendance could only be secured by compulsion. With the onset of winter in 1916, the citizens again brought forward the question of school attendance, and an evening was fixed for the beginning of school. On the appointed evening the Public Works Officer rang the courtyard bell, but on entering the assembly hall it was found that no one had thought of lighting the fire, procuring a lamp, or inviting anyone to teach or form classes. It was clearly necessary to hold a meeting at once to make some organization. The chairman summoned a special meeting, the bell was rung a second time and we assembled to discuss what arrangements should be made and who should make them. Mr. Lane, however, by a question put here and there, now from one point of view and now from another, got the citizens to begin thinking out what was really meant by " school." It was clear that at first the ringing of a bell was considered essential to school, also the arrangement of the classes in

rows in front of a blackboard and a teacher. Mr.
Lane, I think, dwelt on the disadvantages of this
method. Then someone suggested that if you
really wanted to learn a thing, you could learn it
just as well at home, if you had the books ;
quicker than if you were in a class, all of whom
might not want to learn the same thing. The
school law was finally amended into an obligation
binding every citizen to learn something ; they
might choose their own subject and follow it out
in their own homes. The girls chose dress-
making lessons with Mrs. Lane and cookery
lessons with me, and it was at this time that two
of them started on a course with a business correspondence college. Some of the farm boys made
an attempt at studying soils and manures with
Mrs. Edwards, the lady farmer. Mr. Poole, the
elderly carpenter, offered to teach others how to
mend their shoes. Raymond, I think, gave some
lessons in mathematics during his holidays. Mr.
Lane (though the motive for this had nothing to
do with the school) gave three or four talks on
Sunday evenings on the upbringing of little children,
to which the citizens listened with rapt attention.
Then came the spring, with the incessant demands
of the farm and garden, and the " school " faded
away again for the time being. In the winter of
1917 everything was too uncertain and we were
all too much occupied to revive the school. We
were busy planning to reorganize the whole life

and industrial system of the Commonwealth so as
to include formal education as part of the day's
work and not as a compulsory attendance at
evening school. Some of the citizens were begin
ning to be ready for it. John was asking for
something to think about! To Carrie I one day
casually showed the scarlet pistillate flowers of
the hazel and gave her my lens to look with;
she demanded a microscope and more things to
look at, and I began to negotiate for a microscope
and to dream of a course of biology for one or
two of the boys and girls, but the Commonwealth
was closed before any of this could be carried
out. A gifted young student of eurhythmics and
psychology spent her summer vacation with us
and started eurhythmic lessons with the girls. It
was astonishing to see how some of these impulsive
people, with uncontrolled attention, began to concentrate over the music, and to hold their breath
in enjoyment of what they were doing. We had
material there beginning to be ready for con-
centrated formal work, but we were so under-
staffed that we had no time ourselves to begin
teaching, and we had not enough money to venture
on engaging good additional members of staff.

In any case it was not easy at that time to find
people with enough psychological insight to adapt
themselves readily to the education of our rather
difficult citizens. We had one lady, I remember,
who came to us with high qualifications, who, by

way of recreation, told the girls' fortunes in a tea-cup. The girls became more and more fascinated, one or two even wild in their talk about it. The lady did not stay with us long. Mr. Lane believed that if the Commonwealth education was worth anything, the citizens would be able to take any sort of staff in their stride. I am afraid I did not agree, or at least I had not the patience to submit to the lifetime of hopes deferred that this theory involved.

I have said we had a few citizens beginning to be ready for formal education, that is, they were beginning to ask for it and to feel there was something they wanted. Without that spirit, it would have been very difficult to teach them anything. In all my previous attempts at direct instruction in the Commonwealth, I learned to be casual and incidental. In the days of the cooking lessons I once remarked to Carrie that we must baste the meat at frequent intervals. Carrie told me afterwards that she said to herself, " Whatever does she mean by basting ? I won't ask her. I'll watch and find out." I found, for example, that my best opportunity of teaching anything about food values was not in Heather kitchen, but long afterwards, when I was temporarily in charge of the shop, and an anxious house-mother came to buy provisions and actually asked me what would be the most nourishing assortment of food to buy for the family. After months of patient trying to teach, by *doing* things in an unostentatious way and not by talking, I was rewarded by the proudest and most aloof of the house-mothers saying to me as I went away : " If you come across anything you think would do for us here, you might send me the recipes." I think I taught mostly by pretending ignorance at some critical point and turning for help to the excellent housekeeping book I had imported. The result was that a girl or two would occasionally consult the book on her own account—quite a step forward for those who were totally unaccustomed to the use of books for information. If I had said to Carrie, " That's not the way to do it, do it this way," Carrie would have instantly felt that she knew all about it and wasn't going to be told off by anyone. But though it was fatal to be didactic as a teacher, in any other function, as, say, housemother or shopkeeper, one could be perfectly direct. The citizens had acquired, one and all, before they came to the Commonwealth, all sorts of prejudices against teachers as such. In countless little ways one could tell that they were not the children who had been fortunate enough to attend some of the good infant schools with modern methods, and that the schools from which they had so often played truant as they grew older were of the harsh and rigid type, happily not now common, but still to be found here and there, where there are few interests other than those of avoiding punishment or of defying authority. All this instinctive aversion had to be reduced before the Commonwealth school could come into its own. In the ordinary schools we teachers see the children assembled in front of us till they are fourteen. In the Commonwealth were collected together some of the fourteen-year-old human beings produced by those class-rooms. The class-rooms had left us little but hostility or indifference from which to start. The accumulated experiences of nine years had to be dissipated before good will and an appetite for knowledge could be restored.

The devoted and arduous labours of my colleagues in the schools fill me with respect, but I often wish that more teachers could have had Commonwealth experience. If they could have done so, and if they could have understood the significance of some of the truths to be discovered there, fewer boys and girls would be turned out of school at fourteen of such a disposition that only a Commonwealth experience could save them.

CHURCH

The vicar of the neighbouring hamlet served two churches, but he managed to come over to us on alternate Sundays to hold a service in the assembly hall, and on the other Sunday a few of us would walk over to the church. The citizens considered that everybody should attend the service in the assembly hall, but there was no such sentiment about the service in the parish church. This was small, damp and poorly attended; the service was conventional. I used to wonder why any of the citizens went. Ginger, who could not read, used to go, and Maggie, one of the girls of whom we expected little. The services in the assembly hall were a little less remote, but even so it was clear that the citizens chiefly attended out of a feeling of hospitality to the vicar, who was their guest for the time being. As a sequel to the services, a complaint would not infrequently be brought against two or three citizens for bad behaviour in church, that was, for giggling and whispering. The citizens never behaved thus at any of their own meetings and it was quite unlike their usual behaviour. It seemed to me that a white surplice and the recitation of familiar words must have associations for them of boredom, authority and restraint, and provided a stimulus which produced at once the most childish reactions. There were enacted over again, it seemed to me, the wrigglings and resistances of small boys and girls pent up in the side aisle of some parish church while matins wound slowly on. It may be, too, that the associations of the daily Scripture lessons of some of our schools had something to do with the fact that our boys and girls never took kindly to the services. They did, however, always severely censure bad behaviour at church, yet nobody minded when the services were discontinued, whereas everyone would have minded if the Commonwealth meetings had come to an end.

I was once walking along a street in Deptford with a Commonwealth friend. " See," she said, pointing, " that's where I went to school. They never learned me anything there but me prayers. Perhaps if they had learned me something more, I shouldn't be where I am now."

Later, in 1917, the vicar joined the Forces, and there were no more services at the Little Commonwealth. We had previously tried to conduct our own services on Sundays when the vicar could not come. When it was Mr. Lane's turn to select and explain a passage, all listened with interest. But when it came to Florence's turn, she read the story of the feeding of the five thousand and explained that she had chosen it " because it was about kindness, what we want in the Commonwealth." When questioned further as to her meaning, she used the argument as a means of retaliation for her personal grievances. This was felt by everyone to be quite an impossible thing to do. At a later period, I think that Mr. Lane would have carried forward the services himself, but at that time he was very anxious to avoid over-leading the citizens. He wanted them to think for themselves. He would not have hesitated to frame a suitable service for younger children, who, he believed, needed guidance ; but at this time he felt that adolescents would best reach truth, and get away from a merely superficial observance of religion, if they were left to themselves. I think that in his boyhood he had been an ardent attendant at the services of his church. Later he outgrew these. The whole of life was to him a religious experience, and religious observances were left behind as schooling had been. But he felt that they were a natural medium of growth and orientation for youngsters, and whenever he could he tried to make them think about these things, but without success. Though the citizens seemed unable to avoid the topic, they perpetually shied away from it, or left it where they found it. In spite of this, the handful of Roman Catholics went to Sherborne at the great festivals, whilst another handful went to the parish church. The most thoughtful of the boys and the most cruel of the girls and two or three others were confirmed—moved by what divers motives ?

The thoughtful student or youngster who associated with Mr. Lane would find the idea of God and of the Founder of Christianity growing richer and more real in content. The vitality of the idea—once it is apprehended—that " the kingdom of God is within you," may tend to transfer interest and energy from the practice of religious observances to the attempt to follow the Christian way of life. A formal idea, however sound, cannot but make a faint appeal in the ears of those who hear the trumpet-call of Christian endeavour and who have begun to rethink life, both individual and social, in terms of truth, of service and of hope.

CHAPTER V

SOME OF THE CITIZENS

THE TREATMENT. THE UNDERLYING THEORY. EDMUND. ANNIE. JOHN

MYSELF (in a dark moment). I am not sure that I can go on.

MR. LANE. I am not *sure* that I can.

MYSELF. I should like to start the Commonwealth again from the beginning with fresh material.

MR. LANE. It's the old material I care about.

IN describing self-government and, indeed, in observing it for a short time, it is often easy to convey the impression or to gain it that the results of self-government are automatic, that everything just happens, that all that is necessary is to provide the free atmosphere and to allow things to run their course and that good qualities will then develop like the unfolding of a flower.

Those, however, who have practised it, agree that this way of life makes exacting demands upon all their resources of intellect, heart and hand. It is far more difficult than more ordinary educational methods, but also more interesting. Each individual boy or girl is different, no mass application of principles is possible. A fresh version of truth is discovered in each boy or girl, and one has to think over each and watch over each carefully and individually.

When one looks backward or forward to results, the way may seem swift and certain, but the actual development which has preceded results is generally slow, laborious, obscure and often uncertain. The man who tries humbly and scientifically to study himself and his fellow-men, and to educate them in accordance with the truths which he thinks his observations indicate, has, in company with most scientific biologists, to be a gambler. He believes he is on the track of truth, he cannot but steer his course by the light of that belief. His belief is often triumphantly vindicated by the issue of event, but now and again he comes up against an unexpected outcrop of fresh facts, when he has to readjust his knowledge and his practice in order to emerge upon a more comprehensive plane of action and vision. He gambles with all his resources of heart and head and life for the welfare of his boys and girls; he wins them at great price. This is no safe way of life, but is often extraordinarily fruitful. It is only possible for those who have attained complete and light-hearted disinterestedness, and who have identified themselves with the truth as it has been revealed to them.

I have chosen for description none of the outstanding boys and girls of the earlier days, but three of the ordinary citizens whom I knew during the last two years.

EDMUND

Edmund was an undersized boy whose appearance reminded one strongly of the picture at the Tate Gallery of a wistful street urchin, entitled " His First Offence." He was partly French and partly English in origin, with a Cockney stepfather. He was a glib little liar, and whenever the discovery was made that a family larder or the shop had been raided, most people suspected the hand of Edmund. For months after he came to the Commonwealth his work was bad, and he could never be trusted to do it honestly. He was turned off by one foreman after another. There was, however, much that was likeable about him, he was always kind and helpful, he had a sense of humour. At one legislative meeting the citizens were much exercised about him ; he had so many fines, he could never pay his way, and no foreman could be expected to put up with his work. Edmund, sitting there in a borrowed coat too large for him and already in rags, knew less than anyone what was to become of him. " I shall retire and live on my income, I suppose," he muttered. He was quick and ready of tongue, and often made a thoughtful suggestion at a meeting or a sensible comment on daily events, but because he could never be completely trusted, he had not the driving force of one or two of the other boys. On one occasion Mr. Lane had taken over from our lady farmer the early morning muster of the farm boys in the courtyard, the apportionment to them of their jobs and the turning down of those who did not appear to time. It was Edmund, one of the least dependable of them all, who expressed the opinion that " Things will work much better now that Mr. Lane has taken them over."

Later, Edmund got a permanent job on the farm and gradually his work improved; as the farmyard became tidier he himself became steadier. In April 1917 he was one of the first citizens from another house to apply for membership of the newly formed Bramble Workers' Club, and he was elected without hesitation whilst others were rejected. By May, however, he had partly relapsed into some of his old ways. He ran away, was stopped at a distant police station, was fetched back by Leonard and put on " close bounds " by the court; after standing about miserably in the courtyard for a few hours, he ran away again. This time he was stopped by the shepherd at Minterne in a hollow of the Downs; he kept him for a few days until Leonard fetched him back once more. In July he ran away with Jim; they were stopped by a kindly policeman at Tisbury and placed in the union there until I could fetch them. Two days later he was sowing swedes industriously with Jim and Stanley. I do not remember that he ran away again.

He was quite often a guest at Heather on the invitation of the girl hostesses, and a year later he often came to Veronica to play table games with the other boys in my sitting-room. It was Edmund who flew to open the garage doors and light the lamps when the car was brought back at nightfall, after a long afternoon's shopping in Sherborne to provide for the needs of the farm and families.

I remember a comic scene one September evening when I arrived back at the Commonwealth in drenching rain. John[1] the Stone-Age boy of the previous autumn, now with the quiet smile and manners of a brother, took my bicycle away to dry it; Edmund crouched on the hearth and lit my fire, and then went out and trundled in the farm wheelbarrow piled up with more logs, very wet and dirty. Carrie went to look for my lamp, Susan opened a tin of salmon for my tea (one could not refuse cold tinned salmon under such circumstances). All this in the dark, because my lamp, which was the only one in the Commonwealth besides Mrs. Lane's that really burned, had been borrowed, and it was some time before Carrie could recover it. Louie turned on the bath for me and forgot to put in the stopper. In the middle of it all, Mr. Lane came down and scolded

[1] A description of John will be found on p. 126.

me for coming back, and in the evening Ethel came in quietly and sat by the fire and told me she was going to London to learn the dictaphone.

Edmund presently managed to keep his job and to earn a regular wage. His house-mother learned to count on him as one who would always meet his share of the family bills. Then, one day, he told me he had saved 19s. 11d., and did I think I could buy a blue serge suit for him for that sum. On Saturday I went to all the outfitters' shops in Sherborne, and at last was thrilled to find a blue serge suit, just Edmund's size, for 19s. 6d. For two proud Sundays Edmund wore his suit. In another month's time his mother was to come to the Commonwealth on a visit. Then a family crisis occurred in Bramble. Several of the newer citizens had been doing badly, and had not earned enough to pay their share of the weekly bills. Bramble's credit in the shop had been stopped and all the food in the house had been finished at breakfast. The older members of the family, who were earning good wages, put all their resources to helping the weaker ones to pay their share of the family bills. Edmund had no savings to give, as he had only recently bought his suit. In spite of everybody's struggles, there was still a deficit of 13s. 6d., Chicken's unpaid share of the bill. Chicken was an unmannerly boy at that time, who had made himself disagreeable to most people, and perhaps more especially so to Edmund.

Chicken, knowing that he had no money to pay his bills and that no one would be likely to wish to help him, had run away early that morning on to the Downs. The situation became desperate. If Bramble family was unable to pay its way, it would cease to be a Commonwealth family and would become a reformatory house, supported by the Committee, and with rigid institution rules made by the Superintendent.

Without saying a word to anybody, Edmund fetched his new suit, went to the shop with it, said he wanted to give it back, got 13s. 6d. for it, returned across the courtyard to his house-mother and presented her with the sum for Chicken's dues. The family was saved. Long after supper was over, Chicken crept in and up the stairs to the boys' landing to go to bed. To his amazement he found that the score against him had been completely wiped off, that he no longer had to face old troubles, that it was, in a sense, a new family which readmitted him, without comment, and in a friendly fashion, to its circle. I think that the boys and girls of the Commonwealth had deeper experiences of the Christian function of reciprocal forgiveness than some of the eminent Christians in the outside world who, at a later date, were condemning the management of the Commonwealth for not punishing the misdemeanours of the citizens with adequate severity. I am thankful to be able to add that Edmund did manage to redeem his suit before his mother's visit.

ANNIE

Annie was a big, rather hulking lass, from a seaport town in the North.   When I first went to the Commonwealth she was house-girl at Bramble ; Annie in a large, untidy overall, with brawny arms and a semi-protesting expression, was not an encouraging sight.   Many were the complaints brought against her for slovenliness of work and of appearance, and also for not infrequent " taking things " from other citizens.   Neither public opinion nor the efforts of her house-mother had any effect upon her.   She had a heavy, rather lowering expression, and was generally silent and rather sullen.   She was aware of the attacks made upon her, but appeared to be unmoved by them.   She was a continual source of trouble, anxiety, annoyance and fresh effort to Margaret, her housemother, and this continued without a gleam of light for months.

At Christmas-time, Annie, Florence and Irene caused us all great anxiety by running away to Dorchester.   They had intended to spend the day there, but finding themselves at nightfall without money and not knowing the road, they asked help of a policeman and were housed at the police station for the night, until Mr. Lane could be communicated with in the morning.   At the time I was surprised at the combination of these three girls, but it was a combination which was to appear again later on. Irene was small, dainty, quick and sparkling; Florence was tall, graceful, shrewd and rather cruel, a Cockney like Irene, but one who enjoyed frightening weaker people; one who must have her own way, by fair means or foul, either openly or by cunning; extraordinarily quick and glib of tongue and capable of flashes of superficial generosity and goodness. To these two was added Annie, slow, powerful and troubled of mind.

Later on I had an opportunity of visiting Annie's home in the North. It was the typical home of a thrifty North-country housewife. Annie's father was a skilled worker, her stepmother was a small, pleasant, managing woman with straight grey eyes and quick ways. The front room was spotlessly clean, full of furniture and polished brass ornaments. The hearthstone was so clean that the dough for a batch of loaves could be put straight on to it to rise. I thought I could see where the conflict came for Annie in her home. In the North there are roughly two types of people, the long-limbed, fair-haired Scandinavian type and the compactly built, small-featured, brown-haired people typical of Northumbria. Annie belonged to the former, her stepmother to the latter. Impulsive and wayward, Annie found it impossible to adjust herself to the orderly ways and firm rule of her stepmother. She began spreading totally false stories in the district of the relationship of her mother with men. She ran away from home and caused her parents great anxiety, as they feared, I believe with truth, that she was with a man. After a week she returned, and a little later was sent to the Commonwealth in order to remove her from dangerous companions and from the opportunity of spreading fresh rumours about her stepmother.[1]

In January 1917 we had an epidemic of influenza, and Annie became one of the patients of our improvised hospital ward at Heather. Here she suddenly appeared in a new rôle. She got hold of the *Red Fairy Book* and, sitting up in bed, started to read aloud to the other girls. Without hesitation she read on and on, a new light in her face; for the first time she appeared to be animated and intelligent. Any of the other girls would have put the book down long before Annie did.

Two or three weeks later Annie was afflicted with eczema and exchanged house-work for work in the open air. Annie, in blue engineer's overalls, the accustomed garb of the garden girls, was a different being from the uncouth, slovenly house-girl. Her powerful frame acquired dignity, poise and freedom. Her hair seemed to become brighter,

---

[1] After the events which I relate in the sequel, her parents told Mr. Lane that they had not been in the least alarmed by Annie's charges against him; that she had told just the same kind of story about her stepmother, so that they had come to expect such things from Annie.

her eyes bluer, she gradually became more talkative and began to concern herself more about other people. When in the evenings she changed out of her garden overalls into house-wear, she appeared comparatively neat. I remember hearing her mutter to herself about this time: "I shall give up wearing a back hair bow."

What exactly was associated in her mind with the back hair bow I do not know, but certainly with its disappearance began to emerge a different Annie. Still an incalculable power, you could never tell what she would or would not do, what she would or would not be. She had in her the nature of a thunderstorm, at one moment dark and threatening, the next tranquil and with gleams of magnificent sunshine. But the storm quality was always there, we never got through to a period of prolonged calm. With Annie in the garden, Annie's house-mother had a more peaceful time. But Carrie, the garden foreman, herself by no means of a peaceable disposition, soon found herself quarrelling with Annie. Quarrels in the Commonwealth, though fierce and devastating, soon blew over, and after a capricious storm in the garden, I remember Annie and Carrie working side by side next day at the decoudon in the laundry and Annie, after (as I thought) considerable provocation, remarking: "Yes, you're right, Carrie, we ought to do it in such a way" (referring to some laundry process).

During the seasons of ploughing and hay harvest, Mr. Lane sometimes had Annie to help him. With Annie in the hayfield, the other girls' departments would have a period of tranquillity. Added to this, she was of real use in the field; she was bigger and more powerful than any of the boys we then had (the big boys had all gone to the war), and the machinery really needed a second man's strength. Mr. Lane's work on the farm was unusually finished and well thought out. There was mind in it as well as technique. That silent, exacting, finished work in the field was extraordinarily good for Annie; impulsive strength was compelled to integrate itself to keep pace with the almost relentless drive of machinery, carrying out an intelligent purpose. One cannot idle with machinery; if one is careless the result is immediately manifested. That is why laundry work with machinery under Commonwealth circumstances is educational; no personal drive is necessary, the drive of keeping pace with machinery is sufficiently exacting. In the laundry Annie would be working with a possibly aggravating fellow-girl. In the field she was working with a silent and absorbed man who understood what he was doing and was not satisfied with anything short of the very best execution. In the house, garden or laundry personal quarrels might distract one's attention and the work would suffer. In the field there was a rest from quarrels and the

work itself made searching demands upon Annie.
You were ploughing for the future, the Commonwealth itself depended on whether the crops were
lean or heavy. I was inclined to put down Annie's
rebirth to the fact that she was doing this responsible
but slow and heavy work in the open air, away
from the petty worries of the daily household
grind. Mr. Lane, however, ascribed it to the
advent of Jane.

Jane was a large, good-natured, mentally retarded
girl who ought never to have been sent to the
Little Commonwealth. However, there she was,
and we had to bring her up for several months as
best we might until another home could be found
for her. Annie immediately concerned herself
with Jane's well-being; she chid her for her
untidy appearance and helped her to improve it;
she helped her with her work and scolded her
when it was ill done, and protected her, as far as
possible, from the just wrath of her foreman or
the occasional capriciousness of her fellows. Jane
brought out all the protecting and generous
impulses of Annie's nature. Later on Annie was
mothering in the same way a younger boy, Fred,
who had plenty of intelligence but was feckless,
rather mean of spirit and not loved by his companions. It was the underdog and the unattractive to whom Annie invariably extended a
large and sheltering hand.

There came a day when Annie, the once

deplorable house-girl, became a house-mother. The permanent house-mother was away on holiday and Annie was given charge of the house. She carried on very well for a time both on the practical and on the social side. With one sweep of her powerful arm she would scrub the kitchen-table and then proceed to scrub the floor, with a serene expression on her face as she listened to the gramophone which she had captured and set going to play to her from the kitchen " bob-'ole." From the head of the dining-table she would read out the report of the daily inspection of the boys' and girls' landings, and calmly order a boy or girl to go and do what they had left undone before they finished the meal.

But I do not think that Annie was really cut out for house-work, it gave her too little scope for her energy and too much opportunity for clashing with other people. As far as I can remember, Annie was doing house-work in December 1917. She was passing through a restless period and was getting more and more under Florence's influence. Finally she ran away with Florence, and in order to justify themselves the two girls made serious charges against Mr. Lane to the police, thus beginning the sequence of events which led to the closing of the Commonwealth.

Yet at the special meeting[1] in the previous July (1917), when Ethel and Florence had been

---

[1] See Appendix, p. 189.

induced to bring their "talk" about Mr. Lane into the open, it was Annie who hit one of the boys and threatened to give a good hiding to anyone who repeated the lies, and who was only prevented from fighting Florence then and there by the dismissal of the meeting.

Throughout the troubled time of the Home Office inquiry, Annie never wavered in her loyalty to Florence, though she contradicted herself at every turn in doing so. She had a great heart, but she was entangled in the designs of a much quicker and more heartless girl. If Annie could have gone back to the Commonwealth she would have made a great woman. A letter came from Annie to Mr. Lane during that summer after the inquiry, telling him that she could not get work at home and she wished she might come back to the Commonwealth, and anyway she had left behind her the brooch he had given her on her birthday and would he tell one of the girls to send it on to her. But there was no coming back for Annie. The Commonwealth was closing, and that winter Annie was caught in the influenza epidemic and was swept out beyond all human aid.

From the preceding narrative and from the subsequent chapters of this book, the reader will realize the importance of Florence. I feel that a completed description of her is beyond me, and I therefore give here some extracts from one of the reports written by me for the Committee during the summer of 1917 and before the events related in my later chapters. I would ask the reader to form his own picture of Florence from the allusions made to her throughout this narrative and in the document given in the Appendix.

EXTRACT FROM REPORT, JUNE 1917.

The two house-mothers, Susan and Florence, continue to hold their ground. They can, however, scarcely be put in the same class.

Florence is nowhere near Susan in stability, dignity and concentration of purpose. She is superficial and inclined to be frivolous, and she has for a house-mother a quite impossible sense of humour and of what is seemly. But this makes the fact that she is still steering the Veronica ship all the more remarkable. It is now five or six weeks since she began as temporary house-mother, and her ardour for polishing her stove and scrubbing her floor does not seem to have abated—before this Florence could not work well for more than three consecutive days on the same job. Her weakness is that the standards which she tries to live up to and to enforce in the conduct of the family are above her and foreign to her and are, those of the Superintendent. Susan's strength lies in the fact that she has identified herself with these standards, and fights for them as if they were her own. Florence has tenacity, otherwise she would not have held on so long. She has pugnacity, a very necessary quality for a house-mother. Though she has no dignity, she has grace, and even in a dirty overall is not unattractive. In her present crude stage her superficiality saves her from being crushed between the upper and lower millstones of her family and the Superintendent. The most hopeful thing of all about her is that, although she trifles with the day of small opportunities, she responds in a quite unexpected way to the demands of a big responsibility. It is greatly to her credit that she is capable of feeling the exhilaration of having a difficult job to do.

The way in which Susan mothers, coaxes, orders or shakes her head over the boys, including Mr. Lane, fusses over the house and attempts to pacify or compel the girls reminds the spectator of the historic Wendy. She takes her job with a rare and refreshing seriousness, a seriousness so whole-hearted that she has the wit to see the funny side of things and to treat the rubs of family life with the lightness which is their best medicine. She differs from most of her fellows in that whilst they are positively egocentric she is positively objective and at times unselfish. My earliest impression of Susan, nearly a year ago, as a rather dour and unattractive person, is completely effaced by the Susan of to-day, who has a sense of proportion and of humour and a homely sparkle that it does anybody good to live with. I cannot help thinking that Susan has been made not only by being thrown into the melting-pot of the Commonwealth, but by Fate having fished her out of it at the right moment and set her to live again for a time in the ordinary world. She thus got a valuable contrast before returning here. Possibly many of these boys and girls will not come into their own whilst still in the Commonwealth, but probably this will happen after they have left, because it is only when they are once more at the mercy of themselves and the ordinary world that they will be able to see the Commonwealth as a whole and to feel the inspiration of what it stands for.

I have spoken of Susan's unselfishness. It is the unselfishness of the noble savage rather than of the Christian. When worn by family friction, Susan too can relapse into quarrels, and when tired her defence of her idol, the house and her particular way of housekeeping, is apt to become fanatical and her treatment of individuals to be inconsiderate.

This fatigue is a factor in the community life perhaps not enough allowed for, unless one realizes how isolated and forced in upon themselves these town children are by being suddenly plunged into country life. Very few of them really identify themselves with the country spirit; though they have been set in a place of wide horizons they scarcely become adopted into a larger life, they bring with them the short-sightedness of the slum and the self-absorption of those who have always lived in a crowd. This fatigue cripples the advance of the community life, and the chief cause of it is the smallness of the community. If anyone offends another the community is so small and poverty-stricken in ideas that there is nothing more interesting for the injured person to do than to absorb himself in becoming even with the offender.

The smallness of numbers and consequent poverty of ideas encourages these children's already abnormal taste for the most outrageous gossip and increases their inclination for violent quarrels and their tendency to import personal antipathies as a motive into the conduct of public and private life.

Some of my readers will be surprised at the tendency of our girls to indulge in gossip of a sensational and outrageous type. It has to be remembered that the girls were adolescent, and more or less delinquent, and that the invention and repetition of lurid stories is as well-marked an aberration of adolescence as is stealing or running away. It is generally done on impulse and without any preconceived plan, but occasionally some deep-rooted purpose is the motive. Experienced head mistresses and welfare workers who have to do with younger girls in factories are well aware of this aberration and are not unduly disturbed by it, but to those who meet it for the first time, or who have not studied the psychology of delinquency, the stories are alarming and often convincing, as they are furnished with all sorts of circumstantial detail. I could not help feeling in my subsequent brief contact with the officers of the Home Office who investigated the charges made by the girls against Mr. Lane, that they were very much handicapped by possessing neither the experience of the head teacher nor the training of the psychologist to help them in estimating the real nature of the stories. At the Commonwealth we had to live with the girls and their gossip, and we learnt not to be unduly excited by the stories, but to deal with them as they arose. Louie, for instance, was ordered at one meeting to keep out of Bramble, " Because," said the judge, " she makes mischief in Bramble family by repeating things which no one ever said or did."

On another occasion, just as I was going home for a week-end, I said to Louie, " Now, don't have any more rows or scandals whilst I am away, Louie." Louie paused, not in the least resentful, and then, looking quite alert and pleased, said : " Well, after all, it's only once and a while that we do it ! "

We learnt to estimate our neighbours by experience and not by what was said about them or by them. The families might be often troubled by the lurid stories circulated now by this and now by that disgruntled girl citizen, but the girls themselves we knew as lovable, if erratic, people, and the other actors in the stories we knew could never have said or done the things ascribed to them. Whilst young people in the outside world were assuaging their desire for fantasy at the cinema, ours were satisfying the same sensational impulse by the invention of fantastic stories.

NOTE 1.

At the Home Office inquiry the matter was succinctly summarized by one of the witnesses. A distinguished and experienced worker among girls, who had been a visitor at the Commonwealth and had immediately gained the confidence of the girl citizens, was asked to give her views on the stories circulated by the girls. She answered that their occurrence occasioned her no surprise at all, that every one conversant with the ways of delinquent young women knew that such charges were far from uncommon, that they constituted a serious difficulty in work among girls and that one admired all the more the courageous worker who dared to encounter such dangers.

NOTE 2.

An amusing example of a fantasy of a less dangerous type, and of how Mr. Lane dealt with it, is given on page 36 of *Talks to Parents and Teachers*, edited by the Rev. H. H. Symonds.

JOHN

John was one of the boys who came after I went to the Little Commonwealth, so that I was able to follow his development from the beginning. When I first saw him I thought he was nearer an ape-man than anyone I had ever seen, and I wondered whether even the Little Commonwealth could make anything of him. He was large and slouching, with long arms, a drooping head and sullen, dumb and hopeless expression. At first his work was of the feeblest description. I do not remember that complaints were ever brought against him in court for anything other than omissions arising out of carelessness in his work, such as losing the stable broom or neglecting to give Pat water.

By February John was beginning to emerge as a citizen. At a long meeting to consider what was to be done with the non-citizens, one of the leading girls defied the citizens and left the meeting. John, the inarticulate, who had gradually become more stable in his work but had never yet openly asserted himself, stood up and with his head erect said : " Mr. Chairman, I move that Margaret's fetched back again to apologize at once to the citizens and hear the rest of what Mr. Lane has to say."

A little later John injured his leg and we feared that blood-poisoning might develop. Jim and Harry went across the hills to fetch our panel doctor, who refused to come, as it was after hours. Two other boys went four miles in the opposite direction to fetch the other doctor. John's illness helped to educate his family, as, after the first few days, I refused to look after him or cook for him any more, unless the other boys on his landing took care of his room and gathered up his dishes as soon as they were done with and returned them in good order to my cottage.

By the summer John was walking about with a swing in his step, a gentle and tranquil expression on his face, his whole bearing that of a different boy. He had applied for the job of head carter and was doing excellent work on the farm. It was worth while to run to the window to see his horses go by, shining and sleek in the sunshine.

With some of the other boys he used to come and sit in my room in the evening, quietly reading or trying to mend a bit of harness or playing games. He was a quiet and simple-natured boy; his self-respect and helpfulness grew together. The dawn of articulate aspiration came perhaps during the second autumn. John had been playing at table games in my room at Veronica with the other boys, and went over to Heather to fetch a friend's coat, which one of the Heather helpers had been mending. There he saw Mr. Lane, Kenneth, Raymond and Leonard sitting in Mrs. Lane's sitting-room. " I didn't 'arf wish I could be like them and wear a good suit. Perhaps if Mr. Lane would give us some more of those lectures, he would give us something to think about." What a plea for the opening of our school! He realized at any rate some of his ambition later. After the Little Commonwealth was closed, he and Raymond, Kenneth and Allan were left to the very responsible work of carrying on the farm until it could be closed down.[1] Nay, even at once the unconscious process of identification with admired persons began, for I have a picture of him a few days later in that same November, ploughing by moonlight with Allan and Mr. Lane, long after the rest of the world had knocked off work and gone indoors.

Later John went to a gentleman-farmer, but he did not do very well; the farmer could not understand anyone who did not do consistently good work always and all the time. John did do very good work, but with patches of forgetfulness between. When scolded, I could see him gradually going back into childish bewilderment and clumsiness. He left, went home to Camberwell with the present of a chicken for his mother, and later, I believe (in 1919), joined up.

There was nothing strikingly dramatic about John's development, as there had been, for instance, in the case of Ted and James. He came to us like a boy buried, uncouth, inarticulate, childish. In an atmosphere of freedom, of having found something to do, of being left alone, of not being criticized or scolded by superior beings, he lifted up his head, the light came into his eyes, gentleness, common sense and reliability became his characteristics, combined with a wonderful quality of self-effacement. The letters I give illustrate this,

---

[1] See letters on pp. 130 and 131.

so does the little incident described on page 111. It will be observed that it was John who disappeared into the darkness to dry the dripping bicycle, whilst it was Edmund who, with equal sincerity, had all the fun of fussing about with the logs and lighting a blazing fire.

THE LITTLE COMMONWEALTH,
BATCOMBE,
DORSET.

DEAR MISS BAZELEY,

Just a few lines to you to thank you for the paper you sent me as I did not know who they were from well now I have found out I have the pleasure to write.

Well things are not going on very grand down hear at present. we have not had our ricks threshed yet and we have not got all our potatoes up yet and what we have got up 2 ton out of 6 were bad. the onions, beets and Parsnips we have sold the Rodgers at Dorchester and we are going to sell the potatoes to him when they are up and sorted out.

We have got 6 cow milking and send it to the Dairy people at Evershot we only get 8½ gal. a day. that is not much for 6 cows. We have got Mr. Poole's wife and Daughter over here to look after our meals and the are two soldiers as well. but one of them was hear last springs well I suppose I shall be hear for a nother Xmas and that will make 2 Xmas is I have been and not been away for a Holiday. I suppose I shall have one some day. well I think I have said all for this time and will tell you more the next time I hear from you.

I remain,
Your Friend
J. FOSTER.

Autumn 1918.

(After the closing of the Commonwealth.)

THE LITTLE COMMONWEALTH,
BATCOMBE,
HOLYWELL,
DORSET.

DEAR MISS BAZELEY,

Just a few lines to you in answer to your most welcome letter that I received and I am sorry I have not wrote before as I have been in bed with the flue for nearly a week and I have only just got up.

Miss Bazeley I am sorry I cannot come as I have to stop on hear as there is nobody else to cept the place going as Kenneth is going up to London next week as Raymond is leaving as well so that there will be no one left then so I am remaining hear to help out thing. Well I don't think I have much this But will write more next as I have got to help to turn the oat ricks.

I remain Your Truly
JOHN FOSTER.

Autumn 1918.

[*Copy*]

I am sometimes asked what *was* Mr. Lane's method of treatment. How did the Johns, the Louies and the Annies become transformed? Have you ever picked up a sick bird in a cold May, say, a fully fledged young thrush? There it stands, all its feathers fluffed up, its eyes closed, its beak in the air, frozen to itself, lost to the world, drifting on into the next phase of total collapse and disappearance from the world of living beings.

If you take it in and put it in a warm and airy room, if you refrain from fussing over it but leave it alone and go on with your own work, presently it will begin to revive. Its beak will assume a different angle, it will open its eyes, shake its head, give a little chirp, begin hopping about ; then it will be hungry for food, and after it has gained strength and flown about the room, the moment will come when you will open the window for it to fly away.

When I am asked to give examples of Mr. Lane's treatment, I am at a loss how to do so ; I have none of the dramatic narratives of the early days to record. He cured the citizens by living with them, by living a homely, hard-working open-air life combined with deep thinking, a profound knowledge of psychology and powers of very close observation. He had the personal gifts of a delightful smile, a most kind and warm quality of voice, and a complete absence of self. There was nothing exclusive about him nor about Mrs. Lane. They had a delightful family of their own, but everyone in the Commonwealth was a member of the Commonwealth family. There was nothing patriarchal about this family, but the most delicate balance existed of respect and friendship between junior and senior members. Because there was no exercise of personal domination at the Commonwealth, no one's sense of inferiority was excited. Two things may happen when the sense of inferiority is touched ; if a boy or girl with John's disposition is scolded by a superior, he simply draws into himself and reverts to a more childish stage ; a boy or girl like Margaret, Mary, Kenneth or Leonard would have become rebels and revolutionaries; Edmund would have become a little sneak.

But though there was no personal dominance, we were dominated by economic necessity and by the law of cause and effect; individual impulses were controlled by public opinion. Our very freedom from personal direction, our freedom to choose either good or ill, our freedom from anyone to stand between ourselves and the consequences of our acts, brought us up sharply against the necessity which there is in human affairs, against reality.

Many schools are so well organized that nothing ever goes wrong, and no one ever has a chance of learning by experience. In well-organized schools the first piece of chalk, the last duster, are always in place. The forgetfulness or carelessness of a monitor never gets a chance of producing bad results, because some masterly eye sees the omission and the matter is put right before the stage of consequence is reached. At the Commonwealth things were always going wrong owing to the carelessness or inefficiency of citizens, and often the whole community was involved in the consequences.

For instance, Martha left the garden gate open and the cows got in and destroyed weeks of labour. Leonard had used (unauthorized) and spoilt all the Ford sparking-plugs on the pump engine without success, so that the houses were all without water and, the Ford being out of action, there was no means of going to Sherborne to buy new parts. Charlie, the Public Works Officer, had got into trouble during the day for slackness of work, and consequently had forgotten to light the fire in the assembly hall, and so we all had to shiver at meeting in the evening.

Tom had been stealing things out of the shop, and had run away and had been detained by the police at Reading; we all felt the disgrace to the Commonwealth, and had to pay taxes to meet the expenses of fetching him back again.

Mr. Lane was a great believer in the curative power of work, but it was work freely and independently sought and easily lost, not a task set by an authority with penalties if badly done. Many of the younger boys and girls were work-shy, and for months they would be discharged by one foreman after another, with probably a day or two's standing about unemployed in the courtyard between one effort and the next, until in the end they settled down to a steady job. Others would settle down immediately and stick quite successfully to whatever job they had found on first entering the Commonwealth. Some, such as Leonard, would leap to the opportunity for power and independence given them by the weekly wage. Others, such as Martha, would never be entirely independent, but would always need family support. What was the theory of human nature on which Mr. Lane based his work? His belief was that

the driving force in everybody is good, that every
baby is born with a tremendous dynamic impulse
towards goodness and that this impulse is more
than good, it is spiritual.   In other words, every
baby is born with a hunger or craving for perfection, to seek completeness for itself in that
which is outside and beyond itself.   This hunger
is spiritual in its origin, its nature and its goal,
and it seeks satisfaction in different ways at different stages of the individual's development.   It
is the ultimate motive force throughout life and
lies deep down in the unconscious baby's mind.

The impulses and activities of delinquent children
and even of the most ordinary of us would seem
to contradict this belief, but Mr. Lane believed
that all badness is simply misdirected goodness
and that the life energy of many of us has been
turned aside at various stages or partly checked,
so that only a thin and intermittent stream goes
forward towards perfection.

To move towards perfection, it is desirable at
every stage not only to fulfil, but even to exploit
and to exhaust the life impulse at that stage.   For
an impulse which may be spiritual at the stage of
infancy, if it fails to find expression then, may
deteriorate as the result of suppression and emerge
at adolescence, or some later age, in activities that
are anti-social or mischievous.

No child becomes neurotic or delinquent who
has enjoyed freedom in a happy home in early

infancy, but it must be real freedom, both from fear and from moral compulsion. There is always some emotional disturbance at the bottom of delinquency or neurosis. If one wants to make sure of intelligent, happy children who are not afraid to think, it is essential to have parents who love and trust one another, between whom there is confidence and common sense. Again and again one finds in the children who begin stealing or lying that the child's emotional life was perhaps long ago disturbed by the advent of a stepfather or mother, or that the father and mother are separated, or that one bullies or despises the other, or that there is something in their relationship which may once have frightened or mystified the child.

If the motive-force within us is spiritual and if the fulfilment of our development is the love of God, how is it that apparently so very few of us reach the realization of the final purpose for which we were born? Because though the impulse towards completion is in its origin spiritual, it may readily become distracted into something materialistic. Instead of developing creative love, we develop what Mr. Lane called possessive love. Mr. Lane's conception of the contrast between possessive love and creative love throws so much light for many of us on psychological puzzles that at the risk of being tedious I will try to illustrate with concrete examples.

A child of two years was playing with the strap of a railway-carriage window. With complete joy and absorption it continued to fumble with it and to try to force it on and off its button, crooning delighted chuckles to itself the while. A kind old lady sitting in the opposite corner searched her bag and produced a bit of chocolate, and forced it into the absorbed baby's hand. The baby was distracted from its voyage of discovery with the strap and sat still on the seat sucking the bit of chocolate. Thus early in infancy do we distract a baby who is out for spiritual adventures and teach it to satisfy itself with sensual pleasures.

A child of four lay awake early on a summer morning. Suddenly a swallow on burnished wing darted in through the open nursery window and collided with the window on the opposite side of the room. The child scrambled out of bed and, seizing the nursemaid's box for notepaper, succeeded in imprisoning the bird within it. With beating heart she raised the lid and peeped in; yes, the lovely creature which she had watched so often wheeling far overhead was really there, regarding her with beady eye. Perhaps he would become tame and live in the nursery for ever. No, no, that could never be, not for a swallow. The child leaned out of the window and opened the box, the prisoner sprang forth and was in an instant once more wheeling far away with its brothers in the summer sky, whilst the child continued to watch its flight with admiring gaze. How was it that at four the baby made the decision to identify herself with the wonderful object by setting it free rather than by possessing herself of it? Mr. Lane would say that because the baby had not been unduly dominated by her family, therefore her love remained creative, she rejected the idea of the caged bird, and identified herself with the joy and movement of the free one.

A boy may develop a passion for collecting stamps or butterflies. This may remain fixed simply as an impulse to possess, but if the reaction of the boy's surroundings has not cramped him, it will in all probability pass on into a desire to systematize, to understand and to know the natural world.

Albert was a handsome and well-grown little boy of six. In his long-forgotten babyhood he had been an unwanted baby, and his mother had tried to get rid of him by starving him. He was invited, with his little companions, to come to listen to a fairy-story. He came with apparent eagerness, but when he saw that there were no preparations for tea, he melted away and did not return. Tommy, on the other hand, whose mother was a poor but loving and sensible widow, sat with shining eyes which asked for more and more of the fairy-tale, not in the least disturbed because there was no tea.

A student takes the most careful notes of every lecture, another student only takes a note here and there but pursues the subject at every available moment. At the back of the first student's mind lurks a long-forgotten but undissipated fear of the uncertainties and inexplicabilities of life. The uninspired note-taking is an attempt to compensate for the uncertainties of life by amassing the security of notes against a day of reckoning. The other student has developed a genuine passion for knowledge and pursues it for its own sake.

Fear, it seems to me, in its many different forms, with its incidence perhaps so long forgotten that its influence to-day is not suspected, is the most important agent in perverting our creative love into possessive love and in diverting us from what we might be into what we are.

The aim of the Little Commonwealth was to make happy and useful boys and girls. The aim of life to Mr. Lane was enjoyed service.

Did the Little Commonwealth succeed in its aim? I remember one boy who seemed to be quite untouched by the Commonwealth. But he was very little with us, he came quite at the end of the time, he ran away again and again, and was finally sent to prison by the police.

One of the girls, Florence, is, I should judge, not yet a success. But I also believe that if she had not been to the Commonwealth she would be living at a much lower level than she actually is.

Of the others, I should say that they are either already a success in terms of the Commonwealth aim, or an, as yet, uncompleted success. Probably not many of us would claim more than that for ourselves.

CHAPTER VI

HOMER LANE

An Account of Events up to July 1917. The Report Prepared by the Committee

" The world is full of ignorance. Every human being is doing the best that is in him, but that best is founded upon a misconception of reality. Your comments upon acquiescence really involve the technique of teaching. Shall we adopt as a method of teaching the old Mosaic system of attempting to destroy evil as though it were a positive force in order to make room for good, or shall we adapt ourselves to reality (which involves ignorance) and try to make good more attractive than evil ? I feel that evil is merely ignorance, that it is not a positive thing, but only is some previous good that the universe has outgrown. If we try to find absolute truth, we are sure to find something that will one day be outgrown. . . . The funny thing is that unless we recognize the ignorance of the world and love that, as well as the knowledge, we spend our whole time fighting evil, which always fights back, and so there is no energy left for creating knowledge. We must hate *ideas* that are destructive but never *people*, then we realize the good that is always there in everyone. This little sermon is wasted ink ! The whole idea of talking love and service is useless. We only gain ground by living lovingly, which seems to me inevitably to involve acquiescence, but the kind that laughs. Adventures and risks ! Nothing is more risky than loving and laughing. I only feel serious when I try to express my feelings in words, after my work-day is over."—(HOMER LANE, in a letter of 1919.)

As I reflect upon these words from one of Homer Lane's letters, written in 1919, they seem to me to explain much and to foretell much.

What is it which has always made it so difficult to write as one would wish about the man and about his work? I see now that it is the complexity of both which makes the difficulty. If one had known him for two days only, or had visited the Little Commonwealth for a week-end, one might have caught a transmissible impression of them both. But to have worked on the same potato patch for two years and to have shared the sorrows, the homeliness and the treasures of the Commonwealth, is an experience which baffles one with its diversities and complexities. Homer Lane was one who expanded humanity for all who knew him. He pushed back the limits of personality. However much you knew him, you always knew that there were worlds more of him you had not yet had time or capacity to know. And with all the complexity and subtlety of the changing lights and shades which were woven into the Rembrandtesque thing which was he, one was always instinctively absolutely certain of the man. However far he left us behind him, in his rapid turning from one resource to the next, in the deep insight which led him to grapple with the roots of things (which we could only dimly discern on the surface) or in his quite unique orientation towards everything that happened and towards every man, woman and child who came within his orbit, however little in all this we might be able to follow him, yet we all knew that upon him we could always count, that he would never at any time fail anyone.

There must be very few of Homer Lane's students who ever felt for long that they wholly understood him; there must be still fewer who did not feel from the first that he was wholly and completely to be trusted. One would never find a weak point in the metal of which he was made. His spirit had been tested at too white a heat for any place to be found at which it would wear thin. His thoughts might inspire or bewilder his hearers, it was the thinker himself who carried conviction for the nobility and stability of the ideas for which he stood. His theory of life might antagonize his students or set them wondering what he meant; his way of life challenged us all, nay, allured us, to goodness. It had a simplicity that a child could follow, and a humanity, a warmth, a truth and a completeness of surrender which very few of us can dare to attempt. Over it all played a flame of unexpected laughter which preserved for us all a sense of balance and reality when the pathway led through dark woods or dreary and poisonous morasses.

Without any hesitation, he would risk everything dear to him for the least of the children at the Commonwealth or for the most doubtful of his students. He paid a high price for his apparent recklessness, but he nearly always won. It was always of the other that he thought first. During the various crises that beset him, he was always concerned to take more care of his accusers than of himself. When criticism was showered upon him, it was the critics rather than himself that he sought to justify. He laboured to show that he understood them rather than to make himself intelligible to them.

I think that he had extraordinarily little sense of self-preservation, but an equally extraordinary vitality and recuperative power. After many weeks of continuous labour on the farm, combined with the handling of one psychological crisis after another in the Commonwealth groups, he might be speechless with fatigue, but having sat for a spell withdrawn into himself, he would emerge refreshed and ready with some fresh solution for our troubles.

I think it is often not realized how difficult is the process of re-education, whether it is the re-education of the individual by group treatment, as in the case of adolescents, or by individual treatment, as in the case of adults. In neither case is the path of recovery foreknown exactly, nor is the result sure. Our visitors used to speak sometimes as if the straightening out of the personal tangles of our boys and girls happened automatically as a result of Mr. Lane's magical methods.

Other visitors, especially members of the governing body, would speak as if the training of the citizens were as simple a matter as the training of more normal boys and girls. It was truer to regard us first as a clinic rather than as a training centre. Our boys and girls had to be re-made before they could be educated. They had to be taken to pieces by the searching group analysis of family and community life, to be reassembled into a new and happier being by the healing power of the discovery of personal resource and ability and of personal responsibility to the community. We showed many of the marks of dissociation, not only very rapid changes of phases of behaviour, but also clumsiness of manual work, forgetfulness of what had been done with tools, and lack of discrimination in the purpose of things—a pillowcase would be used for a table-centre, an electric light shade for a flower-vase, a window-curtain for a blower for the fire, a table-knife to chop wood. The citizen who had charge of the shop was always one of the most intelligent and most stable of the boys or girls, but the shopkeepers invariably arranged the packages in the shop as a child of five would have done; that is, blue, orange and red packets were arranged to make the prettiest patterns on the shelves, without any reference to their contents. It was interesting to observe that when an ordinary normal schoolgirl took over the shop during the holidays, she rearranged everything according to use and not according to the colour of the wrapper.

The remaking of the citizens was anything but an easy and automatic process. The interesting thing was that though Mr. Lane knew better than most men where he was going, he did not always know how he was going to achieve his end. He had no easy, ready-made solution for every problem. Each individual and each group was a separate problem for study and treatment. He did not always know beforehand what the next development nor even what the final development would be. More than once he felt that he could not go on. But he went on all the same, and by sheer endurance and sheer patience the next phase was born.

During the last two years of the Little Commonwealth, Mr. Lane was working for and expecting the development of a final phase in the life of the community, and this final phase did not arrive. He had all along expected that the very strong commonwealth spirit of loyalty to the community would, at any rate at points, be touched into loyalty towards higher ideals and towards the spirit behind ideals. He did expect that we should develop from communal loyalties towards spiritual ones—and this did not happen.

At the time we accounted for this failure of spiritual growth by the fact that in 1917 our growth all round was retarded by the necessity of

concentrating all our energies on the farm. With
the financial uncertainty produced by the war
pressing heavily on them the Committee decided
not to open the fourth house, not to increase the
community and not to give us facilities for
organizing the " school," which at that time we
felt would open fresh doors to the citizens and
make advance on a higher plane possible. Whether
the bringing of fresh life into the community and
the opening of the school would have had the
result for which we hoped, I do not know. Mr.
Lane came back from a Committee meeting in
London early in 1917 with the news that no
expansion was to take place and that everything
was to be done to make the farm support the
community. From that time we were driven to
the limits of physical fatigue by the war pressure.
We had then no dependable big boys working on
the farm. The big boys who would have been
our stand-by, and who corresponded in age and
development with our older girl workers, had
gone off, as soon as they attained stability, to the
war. There was no boy who was big enough to
do a man's work on the farm ; the consequence
was that Mr. Lane had to do the work of two or
three men, in order that the boys could get through
the work at all. We were all of us engaged upon
a struggle for existence ; it was a hand-to-hand
fight to get through the work of the farm and the
families, for we had now not only to think of the

present, but of the harvest, the winter and the sowing as well, as one does on a frontier farm which has not yet made for itself any reserve of stock or capital against the day of dearth.   As our boys and girls were all town-bred and were all of them by upbringing of the disposition which finds it appallingly difficult to concentrate on any one line of regular action for long at a time, it may be imagined that it was not child's play to run the Commonwealth.   In spite of that fact, our crops were heavier and healthier than those of any of the neighbouring farms, because Mr. Lane ploughed more deeply than any of his neighbours.

We had not much time to stop and ask why the sails of our spiritual argosy did not return, but occasionally we would meet and talk of the lines on which, when better days came, we would develop our " children's university " in our farming community.   For though our crops were heavy and our citizens were developing into fine, upstanding boys and girls, was it worth doing unless the finer fruits of culture and of the spirit could be added to us ?

In his original vision of the Commonwealth, Mr. Lane had always planned for the growth of a village community.   He had thought that some of the best of the older boys and girls, as they became young men and women, would marry, build cottages and form families, and that these fresh young families would be the most valuable of all the forces in the life of the Commonwealth village. I think that without formulating his thought in words he expected that the best of these older boys and girls would experience the same kind of illumination that he had himself experienced in his early married life, and that, with the arrival of the first babies, they would discover a higher purpose in life combined with a desire to make the world a better place for all children as well as their own. The true graduation of the citizens would come with the founding of their families and the discovery of the creative and good spirit at the back of daily life.

As the war ground on year after year it removed from our horizon the possibility of this chance of rebirth. We became a community of younger girls and younger lads, together with five or six of the older girls, who, though childish in some ways, were in other ways young women.

Dr. Crichton Miller has described how there is rather a late stage in the development of the normal girl when, if she has a happy home, she passes through a stage of healthy and admiring companionship with her father. If nothing untoward happens to render her affections permanently dependent upon him, she passes on in due course to the companionship of her young man. But our young men at the Commonwealth had been swept away by the war. Our boys were manly, but they were not grown up. Mr. Lane was the only grown-up boy among them. Consequently, our older girls were not led out of themselves by the formation of fresh and expanding relationships with young men of their own age ; their unconscious life had to turn in upon itself. Consciously they were harassed house-mothers or what not, grappling with difficult jobs under difficult conditions, as all conditions were difficult everywhere during the last years of the war. Their unconscious mind sought relief from the strain by weaving fantastic stories about their own relationships with Mr. Lane. One girl only, Florence, was, I think, in the least conscious of what she was doing and unscrupulously used accusations against him as a means of engineering her own escape from the Commonwealth and from a standard of conduct which was beyond her, except for short spells at a time.

Mr. Lane made no attempt to suppress any of these stories ; on the contrary, he used every means in his power to bring them to the surface, knowing that there they would explode harmlessly and the whole mental life of the girls and the group would be cleansed.

The details of the psychological crises and of the events that followed are given in the Committee's report on " The Closing of the Little Commonwealth," which is reprinted in full in the Appendix and should be read at this point.

CHAPTER VII

HOMER LANE—*continued*

FINAL EVENTS

IT will be seen from the Appendix that the internal situation developed suddenly in its full fury in July 1917. Mr. Lane expected a storm, but not a tornado. I had gone home one Saturday afternoon and returned on Monday, a radiant July day. The Commonwealth seemed unusually silent as I pushed my bicycle through the courtyard, and I noticed Raymond's bicycle standing against the wall and wondered what had brought him back from his school on Monday. The little ones came to my room almost at once to have their hour's reading and sewing, and before it was finished Carrie came in and asked me if I knew what had happened. She told me of the Sunday night meeting (see page 186 of the Appendix) and that Daddy was ill, that he was sitting on the hill-side, doing no work, and that he had not spoken all day.

Mr. Lane was sitting in the shade of a tree, silent and deeply withdrawn, with fatigue in every line of his face. A little behind him was a group of silent and grief-stricken girls, Annie, Louie and some of the others.

The next day he was out very early in the lovely summer morning, sitting by himself high up on the hill-side overlooking the Commonwealth and the blue distance beyond. The rest of us worked all day at the laundry and other chores. In the evening Mr. Lane was sitting, silent and exhausted, in his arm-chair, and I went to tell him I was going to London on the morrow to fetch back some runaways and that I should go by the early train and return by the last. He replied that I had better go by the later train and stay the night, thus conveying to me that he understood that I was taking over full responsibilities during his withdrawal, but that nothing more serious would happen for the time being.

The next day our friend, Mr. Nowell Smith, drove out from Sherborne with a friend of Raymond's to offer help upon the farm. They drove me back so that I could catch a train to Waterloo. I returned the next day with the truants. I had taken a look round the Commonwealth and happened to have stopped for a minute or two to pull up some large and flourishing weeds from a border near the laundry, in the way one automatically does trivial things when one does not know what is the important thing to do. Mr. Lane came slowly along the path on his way from the hill-side into the house. He paused for a moment and looked at what I was doing and my large weeds laid by the heels. " A forlorn hope, a forlorn hope," he murmured gently, as he went on his way.

The next evening was the weekly court. The meeting was quiet and hurried, no one had confidence to dispute anything, nor to impeach Florence (who was in the chair), because a visitor was present.

The following day the cloud lifted. Mr. Lane had a letter from one of the Committee, and he seemed to come back and take hold once more of the present. He drove Mrs. Lane to Sherborne and did the week's shopping. In a day or two he began planning to go away for a holiday with his own girls, back from school, and some of the other girls. But there were still many arrangements to be made at the Commonwealth and citizens' affairs to be straightened out before he could get away. Among other events, Ethel and Florence were reported to have " had a meeting with Mr. Lane and to have taken back all their lies." Florence had previously declared that she would not work at Heather any more, but Mr. Lane asked Mrs. Lane to take her back, and she agreed to do so. It would not have been easy for Florence to find employment in the Commonwealth elsewhere. Ethel, I think, from this point went forward, but Florence was not by any means better yet. Within a week I find an uncompromising picture of her in my diary (August 6th).[1]

---

[1] *Monday, August 6th.*—Susan, the house-mother, refused to give the boys any dinner because their rooms and their landing were so untidy. Carrie and some of the other girls, for their own reasons, did not back Susan up, and it ended in Susan saying she would not be house-mother

These incidents illustrate much that might otherwise be overlooked. First of all, Mr. Lane's amazement at the fury and the extent of the storm which fell upon him and upon the Commonwealth. It was a situation to which he gave the most courageous and thoughtful handling, but when it stood fully revealed to him, it gave him a great shock. When his conscious mind had withdrawn to its inner fastnesses, one saw his unconscious mind still dwelling harmlessly and benevolently among those who had injured him. Still loving beautiful things, the flowers, the blue and dreaming distances, the red roofs of the Commonwealth and the trees of Dorsetshire, where he felt at home. Still considerate for others, and shaking his head sorrowfully and whimsically over the garden, which could not be successfully weeded. His sorrow was not for the calamity as it touched himself, but because we had all of us missed the way. Where had he and we made a mistake that the happy and hopeful life of the Commonwealth should have been driven so far out of its course?

In a week he had recovered and was making

and going to sit in the porch with Florence. Mr. Lane told Miriam to take charge of the house. Miriam was very excited about it. A few hours before she had been planning an expedition to Manchester to rescue her young sister from her father. I had words with Florence over her sitting in our porch and causing trouble whilst her own house was in disorder. Florence hoped to annihilate me by saying, " Miss Bazeley, you are as bad as Daddy." Later in the evening, to my amazement, she came in and said she was sorry and she had been cleaning up her house, and would I come and report on it. Her face quite cleared up, and she lost the dreadful scowl she has had since the climax at the Sunday-night meeting in Veronica a fortnight ago.

fresh plans and we were contriving fresh harness for our ship. And so on to the next crisis, and the storm which blew up this time both from the outside and from the inside of the Commonwealth and which was beyond the power of control of him or of his friends.

The incidents which I have described illustrate Mr. Lane's power of knowing, without being told, what was in a person's conscious mind and also his instant awareness of the significance of unpremeditated actions and events. His mind was so sensitive and lived at all times so close to essentials, that even when he himself was crippled and far withdrawn, he discerned what was significant, and could say the word or two which were necessary for another's welfare. He was able to console and save others in every disaster as it occurred, but himself he forgot. He was extraordinarily quick to react to another's need, but slow to realize his own danger and slow to react in his own defence.

This trait was to appear again and again in subsequent history.

For instance, throughout the Home Office inquiry in 1918, the uppermost thought in his mind was how best to protect the girls from the consequences of their own actions and of the whole proceedings; his mind worked always slowly and unwillingly along the path of making out his own defence.

Once more, at Middlesex Quarter Sessions in 1925, was this tendency to emerge. I had not seen him for some time, until I went to give evidence on his behalf at his second trial in June 1925. I could see at once, as we all did, that he was very tired. When his counsel, owing to a misunderstanding, suddenly and unexpectedly withdrew his case, he was quite unprepared for this turn of events and found it impossible to act quickly enough to save the situation. If he had been defending another, he would have been as quick as thought in controlling the turn of events, but because it was himself who was in deadly danger, he was slow to react. That was his Achilles' heel, he could never defend himself as he defended others. " A singularly pure and unsullied spirit," said one of his friends at the Home Office inquiry in 1918, to which I would add, and strong at every point except just that one of self-preservation and self-conservation ; there danger found him, and we and children and sick folk are daily the poorer for his loss.

After the crisis in 1917, which I have described, we settled down to our ordinary life again with a great feeling of peace and hope. The craze for gossip had been exploited and exploded by recent events and the behaviour and bearing of the girls showed how sorry they were. I think, too, that they were surprised at the storm raised by what was, to all of them except Florence, aimless and random gossip.

Everyone seemed to be trying more than usual to help his neighbour; there was greater peace than usual as between girl and girl and boys and girls.

I, too, was feeling more hopeful, because from this time on we began definitely to plan for an entirely new phase in the Commonwealth development. Mr. Lane felt as I did, that the first chapter in the history of the Commonwealth had reached its natural close. There could now be no doubt that we must replan the Commonwealth life so that cultural education might fill as large a proportion of time and thought as social and industrial training.

The Commonwealth had lived for four years as a working community; now we must replan so that all workers should have leisure, not only for unorganized play, but also for organized instruction As long as the Commonwealth had been in its pioneer stage, the spirit of the community advanced. The constructive work of building up the community, both in a concrete and in a social and ethical sense, had led to a rapid growth of all that was best and finest in individuals and to the establishment of a surprisingly high level of morals and manners in the citizens. But by the end of the third year a pause came; the building of the houses was finished until after the war; our ethical code, after strenuous digging, was, in essentials, composed. With the cessation of the demand for constructive effort, both in doing and in thinking, the advance in the development of individual and common life seemed to slow down, and a period of stagnation, with all the ills of stagnation—introversion of interest, among others —set it in.   A point had been reached at which the citizens took for granted a somewhat Spartan, but breezy, standard of material comfort; they also took for granted a sincere and generous code of social ethics, of caring for one's neighbour and of loyalty to Commonwealth ideals.   Mr. Lane had confidently expected that growth would continue without interruption from the stage of loving one's neighbour to the stage of loving God—that the citizens would pass from a world of social values and motives into one of spiritual values and motives, and thus fulfil what he believed to be the final end of human growth.   But this hope was not realized.   The citizens stuck fast at the social stage; it seems to me that deep down in their hearts they still had one unconscious fear, which inhibited all advance in the direction looked for—they were afraid of God.   Though we frequently plunged into religious discussions, both in family circles and at community meetings, yet the citizens' minds shied off from certain main issues; they shirked going too far at a time in thought; they were, in fact, afraid to think.   The people who are afraid to think are often those who are afraid of God, and one can trace back that fear quite often to the teaching absorbed in infancy that God is a Being who not only sees what one is doing, but sees also what one is thinking. Moreover, this fear is, I believe, not unconnected with the fact that the idea of death is in much popular teaching of little children made to associate with the idea of God. Death is explained as a going to God or a taking by God. Thus our most deeply seated dread may become linked up with the idea of God before we have learnt to associate with Him light and life.

Experience of life in the Commonwealth acted as a group analysis and set the citizens free from many other fears and complexes, but it did not free them from the very conventional and perverted conception of religion that their previous education had given them. In this one respect they were extremely conservative, they seemed incapable of abandoning a conception of religion as an activity, or rather as the negation of activity, in the narrowest of water-tight compartments. A clergyman visitor wore a white surplice and a round collar, but he thought it wrong to work on Sunday and wrong of a boy to ask in all sincerity whether God had made the sin in the world as well as the good. The citizens recognized the clergyman and the convent sisters in Sherborne as religious people from their garments, but they could not recognize the Christian way of life when they saw it. Their previous Sunday-schools and places of worship had laid upon them the routine of Sunday observances so that with religion they associated boredom, obligation and church; but I never saw any suggestion, though I looked for it often, of their associating religion with the Christian way of life, a way of service and happiness, and of daring and beautiful doings. They could recognize the Church, but they could not recognize Christianity, though I think that Margaret had a fleeting intuition of what the way of love and of work meant.

A friend has challenged my meaning, here and elsewhere, in distinguishing between communal and spiritual loyalties. I do not know that I can define my meaning exactly; we felt that the pursuit of goodness, truth and beauty for their own sakes, to use Clutton-Brock's words, was a richer aim and indicated a stage of growth more advanced and likely to lead further than that of simple loyalty to the ideals of the group, though this is good in its degree. We were actually, however, essaying the good life at the Commonwealth partly because of the innate goodness of human beings, partly because, to use a phrase often heard at our meetings, we should be a disgrace to the Commonwealth if we let one another down in that attempt. But this did not carry us far enough. In Homer Lane's view there was, for each individual, an unattained beyond, which embraced at one end social virtues and at the other conscious relationship between the individual and the Creative Spirit, who is the origin and the goal of movement. That beyond is for many still undiscovered, but once the relationship is realized the social virtues are fired by a deeper dynamic, whilst the poise, the harmony and orientation of the individual are never likely to be overturned and are ever being enriched.

The citizens' unconscious fear of, and shrinking from, God, checked not only their complete development as individuals, but also prevented the fuller flowering of the social virtues. Because this fear was unconscious, the usual and familiar approaches to religion were useless. The citizens had, we felt, each to rediscover God for himself, by experience, through society and through cultural and æsthetic education, before they could enter hopefully on the highest stage of growth.

This being so, we made our plans quite definitely in the autumn of 1917 for the widening and deepening of the Commonwealth range by the introduction of intellectual and æsthetic education —it meant a reorganization of the industrial and economic system and an increase of citizens and staff. But here we had to pause; it was the autumn of 1917, when the war was pressing more heavily than ever on all non-military enterprise and service. We had to settle down to earning our daily bread and postpone educational development to that period which no one could count upon of " after the war." Mr. Lane returned to his exacting labours upon the farm, giving a hand whenever possible to each of the other departments; Mrs. Lane's energies were occupied with the nine little ones, as well as with the needs of her own family; mine were completely taken up with duties on the "home," shop, office and laundry side of Commonwealth life. The outlook during that autumn was narrowing and darkening instead of expanding. It was in the dead of this winter that Florence and Annie ran away, got to London and, to justify themselves, made accusations to the police against Mr. Lane. There followed the period of the Home Office inquiry, with its inexplicable happenings and suspensions of happenings, bewildering to those who had no knowledge of the way things are done in Home Office circles.

Throughout this period I was filled with admiration and respect for the citizens. Here was an extraordinary test of the soundness of Commonwealth education. Boys and girls were put to prolonged and searching cross-examinations, minute after minute went by, and he or she continued to answer thoughtfully, deliberately, clearly and truthfully. I knew the boys and girls, I knew every aspect of the Commonwealth life on which they were being questioned, and I was filled with astonishment and pride at the sustained effort of their thinking, at the quiet strength of their mental attitude, at the insight shown in some of their observations and at the candour and freedom from self-consciousness with which they spoke. None of those who sat through the inquiry and listened to the evidence of the citizens could escape from the conviction that if the Commonwealth education could put so fine a temper on raw metal, it was, indeed, worth doing. I came away from those Home Office sessions extremely humble and extremely proud to have been associated with an education which could produce anything so fearless and sensitive, so thoughtful, clean, discriminating and loyal as those Commonwealth youngsters.

The boys and girls who were left in the Commonwealth whilst the inquiry was being held in London, and all through these weeks of uncertainty, did their part too. They instinctively responded to the needs of the time, and were nicer, kinder and more controlled than they had ever been.

The inquiry was closed in the spring of 1918, and once more the Commonwealth settled down to its normal life, or what was left of it, and continued tranquilly through the summer. Mr. Lane was formulating his thoughts on the series of psychological events and was reshaping and deepening his psychological philosophy. He was reading and writing more than usual, and life, for the time, assumed a slightly less strenuous quality. Perhaps we took things more lightly. I know that there was a kindly and sunny feeling every-where. A letter written in May gives a glimpse of daily happenings and of the undercurrent of uncertainty about the future.

LITTLE COMMONWEALTH,
May 30, 1918.

DEAR MISS BAZELEY,

I suppose you hear from some of the people here and so keep posted as to happenings. My depts. (all except the humans) are flourishing. Our fields are *much* better than our neighbours'. (This is sympathy not exultation.) Leonard is doing most excellent work as foreman of the hoeing and weeding and planting of the farm fields. He has eleven boys and manages much better than Mr. Poole. We now have every nook and corner planted and thriving.

Carrie has had a tragedy! She read (in a new garden magazine that I got for her) about insect pests, and the horrible illustrations of the dreadful creatures " Got up in her 'ead." After dreaming several times about these, she undertook to treat the plants as per directions. She got a bucket full of paraffin from the shop and soaked all the French beans with it undiluted. The result is—a scum of lovely petroleum colours on the surface of the ground, the beans having entirely disappeared! I " jawed "! Carrie protested that it was all my fault. I should not have got her the " rotten, lying old magazine." She brought the paper and showed me that the plants should be " sprayed with an *emulsion* of paraffin." She said : " How am I to know what an emulsion means ? You have never taught me to know these long words. Now you see what your rotten education has done to your beans ! "

There is no answer to this, so I have accepted responsibility and sent for more seed, first humbly apologizing to the lady. I only hope that the insect pests of her dreams have yielded to the treatment.

Ethel is now again doing Bramble and, as usual with her, is the sharpest thorn on the bush. (Dear girl.) There have been two violent earthquakes since you left. Carrie and Ethel fought all one day while I hid in the spinney, but after I had very foolishly allowed myself to be dragged into the quarrel (I don't know what it was all about), they made up, slept together, and were inseparable pals. That one lasted a week and there has been one since. Ethel has finally reinstated me as Supt. temporarily, on condition that I go and be analysed to find out what is the matter with me. She thinks it a form of hysteria !

Louie is doing the shop and laundry. Kendle left last week and is living with Ethel's mother in London.

Nothing yet from Rawlinson.[1] It is most strange that they don't pull the trigger and have it over with. I have been intending to go to town for some time, but am waiting to hear from the H.O. before going up.

Yours sincerely,
HOMER LANE.

A delightful and most helpful young married Scottish lady was living at the Commonwealth at this time. She made it one of her jobs to house-mother the helpers. She engineered us so far as to have one helpers' meal a day, when we met apart from our families, either for a late supper with Mrs. Lane, after the labours of the day, or else (an unheard-of distraction) for tea in Mr. Lane's office, in the middle of the afternoon. Mr. Lane, too, was at this time beginning to collect a staff to start the long delayed school in the autumn.

Suddenly, in July, a new and unexpected blow fell. Internal dissensions appeared among the Committee, and they failed to agree upon a policy

---

[1] J. F. P. Rawlinson, K.C., M.P., was conducting the Home Office inquiry.

of development.   One party lost heart.   I believe it was partly daunted by Mr. Lane's use of new psychological terms, partly alarmed by the financial outlook.   The second party welcomed the new psychology and was convinced that funds could be collected for carrying on the Commonwealth as an educational venture quite independently of the Home Office.   In spite of the able leadership of this party, it failed to carry the day, and the Committee resolved to close the Commonwealth.

CRANSTON'S IVANHOE HOTEL,
BLOOMSBURY STREET, W.C. 1.
July 9, 1918.

DEAR MISS BAZELEY,

It's all over now.   At the meeting last night the Com. decided finally to close the L.C. forthwith.

I don't know what the next move is.   There is nothing under consideration, so I suppose the plant and equipment will become just a farm.   I am returning to attend the obsequies this morning.

Yours sincerely,
HOMER LANE.

This decision, from every point of view, was a most cruel blow to Mr. Lane.   I do not think the majority of the Committee in the least realized the significance of what they had done, nor what it meant to Mr. Lane.   I begged him, for his own sake and for the sake of everything for which the Commonwealth stood, to write a full account for publication of the whole sequence of events, together with the extraordinary sequel, but this

he would not do. He could not have done so
without seeming to reproach his friends upon the
Committee. He loved some of the members of
the Committee and would not do anything which
might hurt them. I gave up my attempt to
persuade him, and came to the conclusion that he
was one of the people whom nothing could really
ever injure. He was working and thinking then,
as always, at a level far removed from any where
personal injuries seemed to count, and I reflected
that possibly this disaster would be turned to good
account, if it led to an extension of his teaching
and his practice to a wider circle than could be
reached in the Commonwealth. He quickly turned
from his disappointment to fresh interests and to
fresh uses for his powers, but I think that the
disappointment and the injury went very deep, and
that he suffered very much in the process of
extricating his affections from the Commonwealth
and of going forward with a whole heart to fresh
and unknown labours.

For a long time after he took up work with
grown-ups in London, he hoped to return to
educational work among children. It was in the
many-sidedness of his work with youngsters that I
believe he found the fullest, and to him the most
satisfying, expression of his life's intention rather
than in the lecture-room and consulting-room. In
the latter his heart and head were employed—
with the children his hands were employed as

well. The inventive and masterly doing of things in the workshop and in the open air, exact things with exact and rich results, seemed to me to be the noblest accompaniment, and in the major key, to the profound music of his work with human souls. But his consulting-room work claimed him more and more, even to the exclusion of lecturing. For financial reasons he was obliged to take the work which offered most remuneration, for he not only had his own still young family to support, but the migration to London had involved, in addition to his own family, two of the little ones and four of the girl citizens for whom no provision had been made. After a time these responsibilities were reduced, but even Mr. Lane was sometimes worried, though he never looked it, at the extent of his financial needs.

Before I close this account of the Little Commonwealth, I would like to leave with the reader a picture of the Lanes' London home. It was the London home of any of us who had been at the Little Commonwealth, and I do not think I ever went there without finding citizens there, generally girls, and on Sundays a boy or two as well.

As I turn to reflect upon Homer Lane's later work, the picture comes before me of a child of twelve, racing along the pavement of Gordon Square after a talk with Mr. Lane, crying, " Oh, I'm so happy!" Older people did not do this, but they felt it. Mr. Lane gave them happiness

and power. He made them trust in themselves
and in their own impulses, and thus released for
each one huge stores of energy; by sheer force
of his own good will and sunny disposition, he
redirected those energies, once set free, to constructive and altruistic ends.

To an extraordinary degree he gave people
something to think about. His analysis involved
growth; one had to grow and to continue growing before one understood the full significance of
what he said. He would translate some trifling
detail or effort of daily life out of a paltry individual
value and set it anew into some service or achievement for the good of all.

There was a saying of the Greeks which pleased
Homer Lane when it was applied to the life at
the Commonwealth, that " friends have all things
in common." It was true, not only of the Commonwealth, but of the whole of Homer Lane's life.
He was the friend of everyone, including those
who misunderstood or abused him, and he kept
none of himself back from his friends. He
shared with them an effortless but purposeful
good will, a sensible and sensitive humanity, a
deep, inner conviction of spiritual reality and a
boundless search for truth. Without any reserves
and with the same calmness he gave himself, his
love, and his time to the search for truth and to
the service of his fellow-men. Most of those who
knew him, when they heard of his death, had a

sudden but abiding sensation that the world without him was not so safe as it had been, nor so sunny. Virtue seemed to have gone out of the earth itself when that inexhaustible good will and that inspired common sense were lost to it.

The result and the reward of Homer Lane's life was to have made others better and happier, more certain of themselves and more certain of the creative spirit, which moves and experiments in all living beings towards a great design.

Homer Lane died of heart failure after typhoid and pneumonia in the American Hospital at Neuilly, Paris, on September 5, 1925.

APPENDIX

APPENDIX

APPENDIX

REPORT OF THE COMMITTEE ON THE CLOSING OF THE LITTLE COMMONWEALTH
JULY, 1918

A LETTER has been sent to all Subscribers to the Little Commonwealth informing them that the School has been temporarily closed for the duration of the war. This was followed by a Statement of Accounts and Balance Sheet to June 30, 1917. The Committee now desire to explain to those specially interested in their experiment the reasons which have induced them to close the Little Commonwealth for a time.

Some months ago a grave crisis occurred at the Commonwealth which they have no wish to conceal, since they realize that a full knowledge of all the facts is necessary to a right understanding of the character, motives and actions of those concerned. This crisis, though exceedingly serious and distressing, does not in their opinion reveal any inherent defect in the principles which from the outset they have endeavoured to put into practice at the Little Commonwealth, and which they claim to be abundantly justified by the results which they have enabled them to achieve. Indeed, the difficulty with which they have been confronted will be familiar to all those who have studied the psychology of young persons of the age and temperament of their citizens.

The co-education principle which is carried out at the Little Commonwealth has often been criticized by those to whom it appears novel and unconventional. They have consequently been specially on their guard to discover any symptoms of impending trouble arising from the application of this principle, and they can confidently affirm that they have been justified in the system they have adopted by the absence of any kind of mischief between the boy and girl citizens. During the last year, however, the Commonwealth has been confronted with trouble of a different, though kindred nature, and this has finally brought about the crisis of which it is now thought advisable to give an account.

It should be explained that, although the general principles of co-education and self-government, which are the characteristic features of the Little Commonwealth, were laid down by the Committee, the detailed application of them has been to a great extent left in the hands of their Superintendent, Mr. Homer Lane, who was not only completely in harmony with these principles, both from temperament and experience, when he undertook the management of the School soon after its foundation, but also during the five years in which he has been in charge of it, he has made a reputation throughout the educational world as a profound student of the psychology of children and as a leading exponent of the newest ideas and methods in education. Though in fact the servant of the Committee, they have regarded him more as their adviser and themselves as his fellow-workers in a great educational mission. No man could believe more sincerely than Mr. Lane in the principles of his own work, nor be more courageous in their complete application. His profound Christian sympathy with, and understanding of, all the shortcomings of an erring humanity, and his inexhaustible patience with ignorance, delinquency and all abnormality of intellect or character, have been a source of wonder and encouragement to hundreds of teachers engaged in a most difficult and discouraging profession. One condition, however, is essential to a true estimate of Mr. Lane's influence upon those among whom he works—namely, a generous allowance of time and a patience equal to his own. The process of reformation which he adopts, insisting as it does at all stages upon the unfettered expression and gradual development of the individuality of his pupils, necessitates a much longer period in which to achieve success than does a method which seeks to restrain and correct evil by punishment or to inspire good by the precept or example of the teacher. This essential limitation must be borne in mind by all who read what follows, and accounts for the detail in which the story is told.

The origin of the recent crisis in the Little Commonwealth exclusively concerns the relations between Mr. Lane and the citizens, and the first part of the story therefore can best be told in his own words. The following is taken from a report made by Mr. Lane to the Committee in the early spring of 1918 :

The greatest difficulty to be met in residential co-educational communities for adolescents is the provision of activities for the boys and girls during their periods of recreation. During working hours, whether in a schoolroom or, as in the Commonwealth, in the various manual employments, there is no particular danger that unwholesome relationships between boys and girls will develop. It is after working hours, during the hours of idleness or amusement, that the danger attendant upon intimate relations presents itself.

From the very beginning of our experiment the social life or recreation time of the citizens has been given a great deal of thought and study. My observation of the usual institutional method of providing recreations for children has convinced me that no *organized* social life, or rather no form of play or amusement that is not spontaneous with the children, is really recreating. Institutional amusements are more in the nature of work than play. Any person who has watched children in an institution during their play periods must have noted the lack of joyousness and spontaneity in the games which are played. Nor can play be ignored as unimportant in the life of the child. Play is a necessity, not only to the normal mental development of the child but to moral development as well.

During the very earliest days of the Commonwealth I took up, with my staff, the task of arranging for the recreations of the citizens before that of arranging their work. Instead of planning the exact form of recreations as is usually done, we encouraged the citizens to develop their own form of play and amusement. As is quite natural and to be expected, the boys and girls, with our encouragement, soon showed a partiality for dancing and parlour games. One of the members of the staff was a comedian of no mean ability. His repertoire of comic readings was quite extensive but not very varied. The evenings were spent very happily and profitably with this variety of amusements for a long time.

After the community grew so that there were two or three families, living in separate cottages, we encouraged the citizens to spend more of their evenings in their own homes at quieter amusements and study. A woman teacher was made responsible for the recreations of the citizens. She was always available to those citizens who preferred dancing and games in the Assembly Hall. This resulted, after a time, in the division of the citizens into two parties so far as this form of recreation was concerned—those who preferred the quieter activities of the family sitting-room, and those who chose the more exciting games and dancing in the Assembly Hall. The latter were greatly in the majority.

It was not long before the effect of this was seen in many ways. The rowdy element congregated in the Hall almost nightly, the quieter element among the citizens remaining in their homes enjoying quieter forms of amusement. The rowdies became more unrestrained because of this withdrawal of the influence of the quieter ones.

The Assembly Hall parties, while noisy and hilariously happy, were for a long time quite wholesome and really recreative ; but after a time, having exhausted their repertoire of games and played them so often that they were getting tired of them, a new tendency was to be seen in their parties. The enjoyment of the games and dancing was not, as at first when they were learning them, due to the game itself, but was in getting a *certain partner* for the game or dance. Heretofore the citizens had chosen partners for the dancing without reference to their special friendships. But now there was a decided tendency to remain out of the game unless a certain partner was available. This was fairly general among all the Assembly Hall group.

Then we arranged for a series of lessons in Morris and folk dancing. Miss Neal sent a teacher to instruct the citizens. The result was very satisfactory. The interest in the new dances, while they were being learnt, broke up the tendency to select a particular partner.

After some time, when the Morris dancing had ceased to be a new thing and the citizens had begun to tire of them, the quiet citizens again remained in their homes, and the Hall games again developed into mere opportunities for pairing off.

I had hoped and expected that by encouraging games and dancing to excess the citizens would eventually get " fed up " and be willing to put in a part of their leisure time in school work and reading. But after waiting patiently for a long time I came to the conclusion that some more positive form of discouragement of the perpetual dancing would be necessary. I had also noted that these boys and girls of fifteen to eighteen years of age were playing kindergarten games such as " Drop the handkerchief," " Jolly Miller " and " Winking " for hours at a time.

These games involve no element of " sport " or danger or skill in any form, and while fascinating and educational in the kindergarten, in the Commonwealth were nothing more nor less than opportunities for expressing preferment for one of the opposite sex. This in itself is not unwholesome, and in village life is the chief characteristic of the congregate parties of young people. But I felt that it might become dangerous in that it would destroy the usual delicacy of sex relationship among adolescents upon which we depend for the regulation of relationship between the boys and girls of the Commonwealth.

It would have been easy to have suppressed the dancing and games authoritatively by closing the Hall, but I knew that in doing so that would not in any way destroy the tendency to " pair up." Had the Hall been closed the boys and girls would have found other means to indulge their special friendships, and under much more dangerous conditions.

I therefore adopted a method of meeting the situation which, although requiring much more patience and thought, would, I hoped, be safer and more sure in its final results. Subsequent events, however, did not support my hope.

Whenever cases came up in the citizens' court involving vulgarity, bad manners or rudeness, I would refer to the Assembly Hall games as being the origin of such things in the Commonwealth. It is a fact that for some time, ever since the tendency toward roughness in the games had begun, there had been developing a corresponding tendency toward bad manners and mild vulgarity in the family circles. This supported my contention, but placed the Assembly Hall party on the defensive as a group, separated from the Commonwealth. The citizens divided, more distinctly and definitely, into two parties, according to their like or dislike for the Hall games.

I did not want to suppress the games. It would have been dangerous. I tried to get discussions of the social life started in the meetings of the citizens, in order that they might be *educated* to more refining activities in their amusements. Two members of my staff did not fully agree with me in these matters. They felt that the games were not in any way unwholesome. They very naturally championed the cause of those citizens who regularly met in the Hall for their recreation. These two citizen parties soon became quite distinct, and in the discussion of public affairs in the meetings, resembled two political parties. An election of officers was held at one time, in which each of these parties presented a set of candidates for election. The pre-election campaign was very spirited, with political and party meetings held for the purpose of influencing voters. The speeches, quite naturally, became toward the end more or less personal. One of my assistants and I were much more active in this campaign than we adults usually were in the citizens' affairs, and naturally came in for our share of the " personalities " in the speech-making.

My adult political opponent was a much better orator than myself. I got much the worst of the personal remarks. This exactly suited my purpose, for I wanted to make sure that all those who genuinely disapproved of the form that our social life had taken, and only those, should identify themselves with me. As a matter of fact, I did not object to the form of the games, providing there was an active disapproval of them by a fairly large number of citizens.

Now it was the girls more than the boys who enjoyed the Hall activities. It is a well-known characteristic of girls to indulge in recriminations. And it is here that the tendency of the girls to make insinuations against me began. Whenever I referred to the Hall games in connection with bad manners or vulgarity, the girls would retort in super-political-meeting style, " You're a hooligan yourself."

I may add here that I have always welcomed and encouraged opinions contrary to mine from the citizens. I wanted the citizens to adopt their policies and views because of conviction rather than because those policies are mine. One of the most difficult things I have to do in the Commonwealth is to prevent the citizens from adopting my views and opinions. For this reason the citizens never have any hesitation in differing from me as emphatically and often as disrespectfully as from each other. Only those who have actually lived in the Commonwealth can know how little direct authority I have over the citizens' affairs, community or personal. I purposely and studiously carry this policy of relationship with the citizens to the point of quarrelling with them on their own terms, and in their own terms. I do not adopt a condescending and superior attitude toward any citizen in any sort of relationship. There is no point, in my relationship with the citizens, at which I depart from this policy and resort to my adult dignity or position for protection.

In relating the following incidents it is obviously impossible to use the names of those who took part in the unfortunate events. Fictitious names are therefore substituted.

I was now (about midsummer, 1916) pressing my campaign against the Assembly Hall activities vigorously, taking every opportunity available to discredit the games and dancing as well as those who took part in them.

Florence, aged sixteen, had arrived in the Commonwealth in June 1916. She was committed for staying out at night and general disorder on the streets. Her parents were greatly in fear that she would become a bad girl unless removed from the influence of bad companions, boys and girls. Florence soon became quite popular with the Assembly Hall set by virtue of her accomplishments in the way of grotesque dancing, mimicry and sentimental songs. She had the largest repertoire of typical East London music-hall songs of any person I know. Florence's nickname in the Commonwealth from the first was " Charlie." This name was given her because of her really comic imitation of Charlie Chaplin. My first friction with this girl, of a personal nature, was due to my authoritatively forbidding her to frighten certain younger girls of nervous temperaments by her ghost impersonations. Two girls had been quite hysterical through fright because Florence had dressed up in white and gone to their rooms after they were asleep. I feared serious consequences from this and forbade it.

This girl soon became the chief spokesman of the Assembly Hall set. She was entirely fearless in attacking us in the meetings when the subject was being discussed. She was several times deprived of citizenship by the court for contempt of court. At one meeting she was called to order by the Chairman, refused to submit to his demand, was fined 6d., said " I don't care," was fined 1s., repeated her defiance and so on, until the aggregate of her fines amounted to 24s., when she was sent from the room. In every way, whether about her work or in the meetings, she was a very turbulent spirit. Underneath all this rough exterior, however, was a really nice nature. She was generous to a fault, extremely loyal to her particular friends, and always sympathetic with those who were in trouble with the government.

Her accomplishments put new life into the Assembly Hall parties Many of those who had before her arrival got tired of the games, now joined in the Hall activities again. Those citizens who did not join in the games shared with me the disapproval of the majority. The lady teacher, during all this time, was quite annoyed with me for my constant uncomplimentary reference to the games. She several times asked me if I wished her to discontinue playing the piano for them, or to refuse to join with the Hall parties. I explained to her that I wished particularly to avoid having anything done that would *prevent* the citizens from indulging in the games : that I wanted them to agree that the games were silly and a waste of time. She quite frankly told me that she did not think the games harmful. We agreed to disagree on this point. I wanted the energy expended in this profitless way diverted to school work in the evenings. Twice during the year, June 1916 to June 1917, this teacher decided to resign her position because of the bad feeling among the citizens, and because she did not agree with me as to the policy of discouraging the games.

Carrie Dale was one of the citizens who did not wholly identify herself with the Hall party. She was citizen-garden forewoman, and employed all the girls who were not engaged in other work. She was not always judicious in her management of the girls under her, and frequently was obliged to call on me for help in straightening out disputes between herself and her employées. Florence was a very disturbing element in Carrie's department.

During the winter of 1916–17 personal quarrels between myself and individual citizens were not infrequent. In every case of such a quarrel Florence was active as a supporter of the disaffected citizen. I very soon discovered that she was actively fomenting trouble in the Commonwealth, and that she always suggested to those whom she was influencing that I was unfair and partial. I did not attempt in any way to suppress this tendency, for fear of doing my accuser an injury by making her unpopular amongst the citizens. On the other hand, I placed her in a position of responsibility as housekeeper in Veronica Cottage, where her influence might become stronger.

This action on my part was wholly consistent with my policy of encouraging opposition to my views and opinions. I have never varied this policy, and can point out many instances of a similar kind. The education of the citizens, or of any child for that matter, can only be sound when they are allowed to reach conclusions as a result of their own observation. I wanted Florence to have every opportunity for developing her influence to that point in which its results would be apparent to those under her influence. A suppression of her influence would have merely postponed the breaking out of the tendencies that were apparent at the time. My action in giving her a place of responsibility and influence brought matters to a head very quickly.

By confining Florence's influence to a smaller compass, as in a family, her trouble-making tendencies soon brought the family to grief. The family appealed to me to remove her from her position. This I did not do at once, and finally there was a hunger strike in Veronica, several members refusing to go there for meals.

In May 1917 she had secured work in the garden, where she was as much a disturbing element as she had been in the house.

Meantime, Florence's suggestions against my morality were becoming more and more open. One of the citizen helpers became very angry with me because Florence had deliberately misrepresented a statement I had made in court. This girl resigned her position as a member of the Citizen Staff, and her friend also left her work at Florence's suggestion that friends should stick together.

One day during the time we were planting potatoes (this work was done by the garden girls under Carrie), Florence and three of her friends came to me one morning and said that they refused to work any longer under Carrie because of the bad language that she used. I urged them to return to their work, and said I did not wish them to think I did not object to the bad language, but that since they were not children it was not fatal to them. Then they said it was not themselves they were thinking of but Julia, who was also helping in the work. Julia was a child of ten and frequently helped in the garden work. I went at once to the potato field and asked Julia if she had heard any bad language, and she replied that she had not, but that the girls had had a quarrel which she did not overhear. Two boys who were with the horses covering the potatoes said that they did not hear any bad language. I returned to the four girls and told them that Julia had not heard the bad language, and that therefore they might return to their work satisfied that no harm had been done to the child. They refused to work longer under Carrie, and went on strike and behaved very disagreeably. When I came in from my work for luncheon at midday Julia came to me and said that Carrie had been using bad language in the field and told me what had been said. The child repeated several profane words. The child had come to me directly from the four girls, and I knew at once that they had persuaded her to give false evidence against Carrie. I was very angry with them for not only resorting to such dishonest means of spiting Carrie, but chiefly for having caused Julia to lie to me and to repeat profane language. My comments addressed to the girls left no doubt of my attitude toward those who would do such a despicable thing. One of the girls admitted the error and was tearfully penitent, but the other three were defiant and hard. Employment was refused them by all other departments because of their lack of conscience in the matter, and they were subject to the penalties of the citizens' laws for being out of employment for several days.

During these few days, while they were in this state of mind, they organized the conspiracy that finally resulted in Irene being removed from the Commonwealth by her mother. The facts, as I relate them below, have since been admitted by Florence.

Irene wrote to her mother that she had been insulted by

Mr. Lane; that she was in great danger in the Commonwealth because of this, and that if her mother would come to the Commonwealth there were other girls who could prove her statements.

The mother came, and having heard her daughter's views, was very offensive to everyone in the Commonwealth. She spent the whole of her time with Florence and her daughter. She ridiculed the citizens' laws and ignored the rules concerning leisure time. She took three girls for walks during working hours, they leaving their work undone, wholly ignoring and defying their respective foremen. Irene's mother refused to allow her to attend court to answer for some misdemeanour, and when I remonstrated with her she said that she was taking Irene home in the morning because she was being overworked. She did not mention that any insinuations had been made against my character. I found upon consulting my records that I had no authority to prevent the mother from removing Irene, and was obliged to submit to her decision. The rest of the evening Florence spent with Irene and her mother.

Subsequently I learned that Florence at this time wrote to her parents that I was an " improper " person, and that Irene's mother would corroborate the assertion. She requested her parents to remove her from the Commonwealth.

Finally, as I had expected and hoped, Florence's activities became noticeable and were felt throughout the Commonwealth. But the effect was much more serious than I had anticipated. She had succeeded in convincing Ethel Moore that I was a bad man. There was general gossip about me. Ethel, in a manner that is characteristic of her, became more active in the gossip and talk than anyone had been before. At that time Ethel was conspicuous in the community because of her partiality for one of the boys. I was, as usual, making their relationship as conspicuous as possible. Ethel was angry with me because of this, and joined with Florence in her agitation against me. I discovered that there was an entirely new tendency on the part of the boys and girls to get together in small groups, but on my approach to discontinue their conversation and go away in a conspicuously self-conscious manner. Ethel, with her superior ability, and because she was a respected citizen, strengthened Florence's cause enormously, and I could clearly see that the climax of this long-drawn-out contest was close at hand. Florence, now triumphant, became bolder in her methods. She had never said anything about herself to my discredit. Her method was always to get others to make insinuations, and then, when she had been successful, to pretend that she had tried to discourage the talk. In almost every case where there had been any unwholesome gossip, Florence was the one who told me about it with a pretence of regret and virtue.

One Friday evening in court, during my absence from the Commonwealth, Florence and her supporters were particularly offensive. This was early in July. Insinuations were, from all accounts, quite open that I was not treating the citizens fairly, that I was partial towards certain ones, that I must have reasons for this, etc.

On my return I determined to work the situation up to a crisis during the week so that there could be an exposé of the situation as early as possible. The relationship between the boys and girls was becoming too dangerous to be allowed to continue. It was an exceedingly delicate situation. A false step at this point would have been disastrous to the Commonwealth. The evil influence that had been at work for nearly a year had brought the Commonwealth to the most dangerous and critical point in its history. If my plans did not miscarry I felt that never again would we have to meet such a critical situation, and the sum total of the experience through which the community was passing would live for ever as a lesson to the future as well as the present citizens. I was careful to avoid doing anything that would prevent the achievement of my object, which was a dramatic exposé of the conspirators.

I remained wholly passive during the week, taking no part in the agitation other than to continue my surveillance of the groups of boys and girls, and to show wordless annoyance of these gatherings.

On Friday evening, in court, there was a continuation of the quarrelling of the previous week. The citizen judge was unable to carry on his work, and the meeting was at the point of breaking up in confusion, when I got the floor and made a speech. I pointed out to the citizens the impossibility of going on under the present conditions. I described how the work of the different departments had suffered because of the continuous quarrelling; how the courts and meetings had become a disgrace to the name Commonwealth; how the family life and social life had suffered; how no one in the community could possibly be happy under the present conditions, and concluded by stating that unless some remedy could be found for the conditions, it would be quite impossible for the Commonwealth to continue its existence as a citizen-governed community. I stated that there were certain persons in the room who seemed to enjoy the present situation, as shown by their behaviour, but that it was evident that the majority were thoroughly disgusted with the situation. Could anyone tell where the weak spot was? There certainly was one somewhere and it must be found.

The citizens were sobered by my speech, and after a short discussion decided, as it was late, to adjourn the meeting until Sunday evening, when there would be an attempt to find the defect in the community.

There was a good deal of discussion of the situation during the next day, the citizens seeming to be quite anxious to find the trouble and eradicate it.

Ethel seemed worried, but Florence appeared to be quite jubilant. When the adjourned meeting was called to order by the chairman, Ethel, Florence and one of the boys were not present, but were finally compelled to attend.

A discussion of the trouble finally led to the decision that the defect centred around the two girls who were disturbing the whole community by their underhand methods.

One of the citizens said that it was no wonder that the

Commonwealth was "rotten" when there were people like Florence and Ethel in it. Ethel then said angrily, "We are not the rotten spot in the Commonwealth, but I can tell you where it is if you want to know." She was challenged to say where it was from several parts of the room. She only kept repeating her assertion. There were several speeches by different citizens offering suggestions as to what might be done to discover the rotten spot, most of which were directed against Ethel. It was very noticeable all through this meeting that Florence had nothing to say, but kept whispering to Ethel, who did all the talking.

There seemed to be no likelihood of matters coming to a head if left wholly to the citizens, so after a time I pressed Ethel to state what, in her opinion, was the matter with the Commonwealth. She only vaguely hinted that I had better look out or she would tell. I challenged her to tell. She sat down and refused to speak. The chairman appealed to her to either tell what she had said she could tell, or withdraw her statement that she knew what was the matter with the Commonwealth here ; but she added that she would tell some time. She was pressed from all sides to tell until she finally said she would tell one of the women-helpers some time after the meeting. She was asked to retire with her at once and tell, so that we could get on with the meeting. She refused to do this. I pressed the matter, but she still said she would not tell anything until the meeting was closed.

I was bitterly disappointed at this turn of events, but could think of no way to force the matter to such a point as would enable me to bring up the relationship between the boys and the girls, and to discuss the gossip that they had been indulging in.

Soon after this meeting was concluded I was told by my assistant that the girls had made accusations of impropriety against me. I immediately requested the citizens to re-assemble.

The chairman called the meeting to order and said: "Mr. Lane has asked for this meeting, because Florence and Ethel have found out what is the matter with the Commonwealth." There was a long silence except for asides in an undertone by various citizens, such as : " Everyone knows that. What is the use of getting out of bed for that ?" " If they know, why don't they stop swanking ?" etc.

Several boys attempted to leave the room, but were prevented by the chairman.

I feared that nothing would come of the meeting, and said that as the girls had promised to let the citizens know what was the matter with the Commonwealth, could they not be compelled to do so ? Neither spoke. The Chairman said : " Will you tell what is the matter with the Commonwealth ? " Neither would speak.

After considerable pressure from all sides, in which I joined, without any result, I asked my assistant whom the girls had talked with if she would state to the citizens what the girls had told her. This she refused to do. I then asked her if it was true that the girls had been to her and stated that I had behaved improperly to them. She replied in the affirmative. I proceeded to question her further as to exactly what they had said, but was prevented by the uproar of disapproval and indignation which was directed towards the girls from every quarter of the room. The chairman failed to get order. I was amazed at the situation, for it now appeared beyond doubt that there had been a quite general discussion among nearly all the citizens during the previous week about the insinuations made against myself.

Florence and Ethel withdrew to a far corner of the room and seemed frightened at the commotion they had caused. They remained quiet during the greater part of the meeting. I directed my efforts towards getting them to state their charges publicly, but they refused. Finally, when sufficient quiet had been restored so that one could be heard, one after another of the boys accused these girls and several others of having told them " things " about myself. There was no indelicacy in the matter of words and terms used during the entire meeting, but there was no doubt as to the matter that improper conduct on my part was meant. With the exception of two boys, every person in the room was hurling invective at the girls who had been talking during the past few days. There were several threats of personal violence toward those girls who had been gossiping, and toward the two boys who supported Florence and Ethel. The meeting continued for about two hours, several citizens, bored by the constant repetition of charges and counter-charges, leaving from time to time to go to bed.

I pressed continuously for definite statements, but the two girls, now entirely subdued and apparently frightened, refused to speak. Finally, after all were in a state of nervous exhaustion, I realized that by any method employed up to the present it would be impossible to secure a confession from the girls that they had made up the lies for a purpose. This was the point that must be reached somehow, else the meeting and the plans for it that I had been making for so long had failed of its purpose.

I then stated that if the girls intended that their accusations against me were of a serious nature, so serious that it made me a criminal, then obviously the citizens' court could not take up the matter and it would have to be brought before an outside Court.

" How do you mean ? " asked Florence.

" By going to the local police and making your accusations against me to them," I replied.

Then a most remarkable thing happened. Both girls seized upon my suggestion eagerly and affirmed at once that they proposed to adopt this course. I encouraged the proposal. Then there was such a tumult of bitter anger against Florence and Ethel that I feared for them, and tried to quieten the disorder and protect the two girls.

Ethel was now very quiet and certainly sick of the whole thing, but Florence was more excited than ever. She had seized upon my suggestion about the police as a possible means of securing her end even yet. She was in a state of excitement and hysteria that was alarming.

Bitterly disappointed that the meeting had failed to bring about a public confession from the girls that their stories were a tissue of lies, I secured a promise from all the citizens that they would not continue the quarrel after the meeting, promised the girls that I would take them to Cerne the following morning to the police, and asked the chairman to close the meeting.

I had failed in my purpose, and it was a most bitter disappointment. It was now about two in the morning. I left the meeting ahead of the others, with a sense of utter exhaustion and worry for fear of violence against the two girls. I had for weeks been doing the most exhausting manual labour on the farm, working from fourteen to eighteen hours daily. The meeting, while wholly successful from the point of view of clearing up the dangerous situation between the boys and girls, wholly satisfying everyone in the community that there was no truth in the insinuations against myself, was now left in such a way that the two girls were in a great difficulty. I could not see how they were to ever get re-established in the Commonwealth. The feeling against them was so bitter that I did not think it possible for them to be able again to take their places as citizens. The punishment for them had been too severe, and I blamed myself for not having foreseen that their pride would never permit them to make a confession and to resume their life afresh.

After reaching my room I fell ill. It was several days before I was sufficiently recovered to realize that the meeting had failed to wholly clear up the matter. Both girls had now entirely changed in their attitude toward me because of my illness. They were most kind and considerate.

It was now too late to finish the matter of the late meeting. I had hoped to be able to carry the matter to the point at which the girls would admit the whole conspiracy and get it off their minds. My illness prevented the final conclusion of this unfortunate affair. However, the public discussion of the gossip that Florence had started completely corrected the dangerous conversations between the boys and girls.

Florence and Ethel became unpopular and both seemed penitent.

Ethel meantime had been subscribing to a course in office training with a correspondence school. She was ambitious, keen and bright. An opportunity for her to apply her knowledge of bookkeeping, etc., soon presented itself by the resignation of one of the staff. Ethel, who was now finished with her two years' enforced residence in the Commonwealth, was appointed to the vacancy. It was necessary, however, to provide additional equipment for the office owing to her lack of experience. I found a second-hand dictaphone that could be secured as a help to her inexperience in shorthand, and I took her to London to learn the use of the machine and also to go over office details with our London accountant.

Ethel had no suitable friend with whom she could stay in London, and I therefore secured a room for her at the hotel where I always stay when in London. She was in London two days attending to her work. On one evening I took her to a theatre, the Haymarket.

In August I was compelled by my physician to take a rest. I have always made it a point to provide changes or holidays for those citizens whose homes are such that they cannot visit them safely. The life in the Commonwealth is so intense that every citizen should have a brief holiday away from the care and responsibilities of citizenship. This is especially true of the older girl citizens who assume the larger and more trying responsibilities as members of the citizen staff.

I therefore invited Ethel and two other girls to go with my daughter and myself to Torquay on this holiday. We all had rooms at the same hotel. We engaged tents at a remote and quiet point near Paignton and spent our time there, returning at night to our hotel.

All three girl citizens were graduate citizens doing responsible executive work, and none of them could have gone to their homes for a change. All three had been planning a holiday unattended, and had I not provided for it under my own supervision, they would have gone unattended to some place that might not have been wholly good for them. This holiday was no new departure. I would also point out to those who consider such a procedure as imprudent, that my daughter was one of the Torquay party.

The fact that Ethel, who had but recently made the accusations against me, was a member of the party has been judged as damaging to my defence against the charge of being indiscreet. However this may be, the fact is that the unpleasantness of July did not occur to me as affecting the inclusion of Ethel in this holiday party. One who knows the stress of emotion that prevails during adolescence does not visit permanent punishment and disapproval for hysterical actions, however serious may be their consequences.

It appears to me that the first principles of Christianity and of teaching children both demand that a fault of a child should not be a hindrance to the warmest and most cordial of relationship. My own view of the Torquay holiday is that the inclusion of Ethel in the party has no bearing whatever on the truth or falsehood of any offence she may have committed against myself previously.

The impropriety of the holiday itself is a matter of convention quite new to me.

In December Florence again became unsettled owing to her unpopularity and she absconded, going to London, where she was arrested and held until I could send for her. Upon being taken to the police station and questioned, she was very penitent for having run away and urged that she might be allowed to return of her own accord, unattended. She was so evidently sorry for her hasty action that the officers were very favourably impressed with her sincerity and would have yielded to her request had I not already wired that I was on the way to fetch her.

A fortnight later she again absconded with another girl and two boys after robbing the office safe. After about a week, during which time she was living at home with her girl friend, she was again taken into custody by the same officers whom she had impressed by her evident sincerity on the previous occasion. To justify her more serious offence against the Commonwealth in robbing the safe and absconding with boys, she was impelled to find some excuse that would be sufficient to cover such serious conduct. She secured the promise of her friend to support her charges against me, made them, and precipitated the disaster that has now befallen the Commonwealth.

The complete, though fortunately only temporary, nervous breakdown of Mr. Lane, produced by the strain of the agitating events in July 1917, had important consequences—some good and some bad. On the one hand, it helped the citizens to recover from the stormy period they had passed through. There was a complete cessation of the gossip between the boys and girls. Both were on their best behaviour, and those who had been responsible for the mischief seemed to have but one thought—to make amends for the past and to play up both in their work and in their social relationships. On the other hand, it prevented the consummation of Mr. Lane's purpose in holding the citizens' meetings and forcing to the surface the unhealthy gossip which had been going on. As he has himself explained, he was greatly disappointed at not securing at the meeting a confession from his accusers that their charges were false, and his suggestion of carrying the matter to the police court could not be carried out. What is even more unfortunate, it prevented him from reporting at once to the Committee what had occurred. After his recovery the whole atmosphere had so completely changed that he was reluctant to revive an incident which he considered closed, and feared that an investigation by the Committee would revive matters which everyone seemed anxious to forget. The Committee, however, cannot acquit Mr. Lane of blame in this respect, as they feel that a thorough investigation at the time might have prevented the aggravated crisis which followed.

It was not till October that the Executive Committee heard of the circumstances in which Irene had been withdrawn from the Little Commonwealth. Her mother was interviewed in London by two members of the Committee, and on being asked to state the specific nature of the charge, admitted fully that she did not take the matter seriously. Three members of the Committee then visited the Commonwealth and took considerable pains to investigate the matter for themselves. They could find no evidence at that time of the continuance of any trouble, and Florence, who had throughout been the instigator of all the gossip and the ringleader of the disaffected groups, volunteered the admission that it was all " nonsense " and had now been forgotten.

On the night of December 30, 1917, as already related by Mr. Lane, Florence and Annie with two boys gained access to the safe in the office, robbed the contents and afterwards ran away from the Commonwealth. When they got beyond the precincts they separated. The two boys were arrested the next day and brought back to the Commonwealth. The two girls made their way to London, where they spent about a week together before they were discovered. On being taken to the police station, where they found themselves under the obligation to justify their action, they both asserted that they had run away because of Mr. Lane's conduct towards them.

Florence, who had assured the Committee in October that her previous charges were untrue, and who a fortnight before had made no accusations against anyone in this same police court, now declared that Mr. Lane had acted indecently towards her on two occasions. Annie, who in the previous July had most stoutly resented the charges brought by the other girls, now went further and stated that Mr. Lane had had immoral connection with her.

The matter was reported to the Home Office by the police, and, after interviews had been held with the Officials and a statement put in writing by Mr. Lane, the Committee were informed that the Home Secretary had been advised to withdraw from the Little Commonwealth the certificate which had been granted in March 1917. On January 22nd the General Committee met to discuss the communication which had been received from the Home Office, and to hear the report of the Executive on the matter. After a long discussion the Committee unanimously passed a vote of confidence in Mr. Lane, and assured him of their indignation at the vile charges which had been brought against him, which they were convinced were false and malicious. It was also agreed that a deputation from the Committee should call on the Home Secretary and give him the necessary explanation.

On January 24th Lord Sandwich, Lord Lytton, Mr. Chapman and Mr. Hawker went to see Sir George Cave, and represented to him their conviction of the falsehood of the charges. To withdraw the certificate in these circumstances would, they contended, be an act of grave injustice. They asked that judgment might be suspended until the Committee had had time to investigate the matter fully and make a report, and they requested that Dr. Norris, the Chief Inspector of Reformatory and Industrial Schools, might be associated with them in the investigation in order that the Home Office interests might be considered. To this the Home Secretary agreed, and the first meeting was fixed for the following evening.

The next day, however, a letter was received from Sir George Cave stating that he had decided to hold a private inquiry into the management of the Little Commonwealth, " including, of course, the charges which have been brought against the superintendent," and that pending the result of this inquiry it was not advisable that Dr. Norris should take any part in their deliberations. As the Committee was most anxious that the whole matter should receive the fullest possible investigation, they welcomed this decision. At the same time they were apprehensive lest the result of the inquiry should be prejudiced by a lack of sympathy with the unconventional methods of co-education and self-government which were the special features of their work. Accordingly, on January 28th, Lord Lytton addressed the following letter to Sir George Cave :

HOUSE OF LORDS,
Jan. 28, 1918.

DEAR SIR GEORGE,

Since I saw you on Friday, we have had another discussion about the course which you propose to adopt in the matter of the Little Commonwealth. We are very glad of your decision because we feel convinced that only the fullest possible inquiry can clear up the very serious matters that are now in suspense. We are, however, very seriously concerned at the harmful effect which must be produced upon the minds of the girls if they are again questioned and cross-examined privately and separately with a view to obtaining *evidence* of the alleged acts. Moreover, some of the questions that would be necessary could not well be put by a man.

Again, as an examination into and understanding of the principles and methods of management adopted by the Commonwealth is necessary to the clearing up of the charges, we are very concerned that that part of the inquiry should be thorough and unprejudiced.

We therefore wish to suggest for your consideration the appointment of three persons to conduct the inquiry :

(1) A man to be nominated by the Home Office.
(2) Another man to be suggested by ourselves for the approval of the Home Office.
(3) A woman probation officer who could question the girls, should this be thought necessary, about the details of the charges which have been made.

Perhaps you have already made your selection and drawn up your terms of reference, but if not I should be grateful if you would give the above suggestion your consideration.

Of course the person whom we should suggest would not be anyone who has any connection whatever with the Commonwealth, but merely someone whom we should feel was capable of understanding the principles on which it has been established.

If you think that we are not entitled to have any voice

in the selection of the *personnel* of the inquiry, I would still ask you to appoint three persons, or at least two, rather than place the whole responsibility upon one man.

I am,

Yours sincerely,

LYTTON.

No answer was received to this letter, the Home Secretary having, in fact, appointed Mr. J. F. P. Rawlinson, K.C., M.P., that same day to conduct the inquiry. The Committee were not made acquainted with this decision until after Mr. Rawlinson had actually left London to commence the task entrusted to him, and they were therefore given no opportunity of discussing the time, place or nature of the procedure which it was proposed to adopt. Mr. Rawlinson proceeded to Dorchester under the impression that everything had been arranged by the Home Office for the inquiry to commence there on Wednesday, January 30th. Mr. Lane was at that time in London conferring with the Committee, and as soon as they heard that Mr. Rawlinson had left London he returned to the Little Commonwealth, expecting that the inquiry would be commenced there. On Thursday afternoon, the 31st, he received a brief visit from Mr. Rawlinson, who informed him that the proceedings would commence at the King's Arms Hotel in Dorchester the following morning, and left with him a list of the persons whom he desired to attend. Two sittings took place in the hotel. On finding that none of the members of his Committee could be present at Dorchester, Mr. Lane pressed strongly for the inquiry to be adjourned to London, and his request was finally granted on Saturday, February 2nd.

The inquiry was resumed at the Home Office on the following Friday, February 8th. On that occasion and throughout the subsequent proceedings four members of the Committee, Lord Sandwich, Lord Lytton, Mr. Cecil Chapman and Mr. Hawker, were present and heard the evidence. The hearings took place on February 8th, 9th, 22nd, 23rd, 25th, April 4th and 5th. As the proceedings were private, nothing can be said about them, but those members of the Committee who were present had every reason to be satisfied with the straightforward manner in which the citizens gave their evidence. Only one of the girls who had made charges at the police court was examined. The other one had disappeared, having run away from the institution to which she had been committed and could not be found. Mr. Lane was present throughout the proceedings and was examined at length. The members of the Committee who attended were also heard, and they were able to report to their colleagues subsequently that they were more firmly convinced than ever, as the result of the proceedings, of the perfect innocence of Mr. Lane.

The inquiry terminated on April 5th, but it was not till June 6th that any result was communicated to the Committee. On that day Lord Sandwich received the following letter from the Home Office :

HOME OFFICE, WHITEHALL,

MY LORD, *June 6, 1918.*

I am directed by the Secretary of State to say that he has now received from Mr. Rawlinson, K.C., his report on the inquiry as to the " Little Commonwealth," and he regrets to inform the Committee that in view of the terms of the report it is impossible for him to continue the certificate of the " Little Commonwealth " if it remains under the superintendence of Mr. Homer Lane.

If, however, the Committee will appoint another superintendent, and will make certain modifications in the arrangements and methods which will be indicated to them by the Chief Inspector of Reformatory and Industrial Schools, Sir George Cave will be glad to continue the certificate.

I have the honour to be,
My Lord,
Your Lordship's obedient Servant,
EDWARD TROUP.

The Right Honourable
The Earl of Sandwich,
12 Rutland Gate, S.W. 7.

The receipt of this letter placed the Committee in a very difficult position. While they viewed with regret the fact that on occasions Mr. Lane, in disregarding the ordinary conventions, had shown certain indiscretions, they were unanimously convinced of his innocence. That being the case, they could not accept the Home Secretary's conditions for the continuance of his certificate, which obviously implied Mr. Lane's guilt.

To have carried on the Little Commonwealth with Mr. Lane in charge, on the other hand, in the face of the withdrawal of the certificate by the Home Office, presented a combination of difficulties which, in the opinion of the members of the Committee, with one exception, rendered the task an insuperable one.

These may be summarized as follows :

1. The Committee had reason to believe, in view of what had occurred, that they might be met with official opposition.

2. They would undoubtedly have suffered from the difficulty of obtaining children sent from the police courts under the Probation Act owing to magistrates being informed of the withdrawal of the certificate.

3. It would have been incumbent upon the Committee to have informed prospective parents of children sent either from police courts or by private arrangement, of the facts, with the result that the development of the work would have been disadvantageously affected.

4. The loss of grants from the Home Office and Local Authorities through the withdrawal of the certificate, on the top of the ever-increasing difficulty of obtaining private subscriptions and donations, further added to the already existing financial indebtedness. Indeed, some time previously to the Home Office inquiry, the Committee had under serious consideration the possibility of being unable to continue its work on this account.

5. Obtaining adequate staff in war time, resulting in a loss of general efficiency, was a further problem that had for a considerable length of time troubled the Committee.

Faced with these many difficulties, after long deliberation the Committee came to the conclusion, with the greatest reluctance, that no other course was open to them except to close the Little Commonwealth for the duration of the war.

They have every intention of reopening it when the war is over and when conditions are more favourable for securing an adequate income and a sufficient staff to deal with all the phases of this educational experiment.

The bare announcement in the Press that the Little Commonwealth has been closed has already produced a large number of sympathetic inquiries. It is in answer to those that this statement has been prepared with a full sense of the Committee's responsibility in the matter, and also with confidence that those who know Mr. Lane will read it with understanding and sympathy. It is not the first time that an honest, upright and courageous man in the exercise of a noble work among neurotic and delinquent children (such as the Little Commonwealth was bound to receive) has been threatened with the blasting of his work. Every book on psychology makes reference to this danger, and the experience of many who will read this story will supply illustrations of a similar kind. The Committee now leave to a wider tribunal than the private hearing by which alone it has at present been judged the reputation of one from whom many besides themselves have received encouragement and inspiration in their work.